D0828368

BANGKOK

BANGKOK

TEXT BY
WILLIAM WARREN
PHOTOGRAPHS BY
MARC RIBOUD

WEATHERHILL / SERASIA
NEW YORK · TOKYO · HONG KONG

First Edition, 1972

Jointly published by John Weatherhill, Inc., 149 Madison Avenue, New York, New York 10016, with editorial offices at 7-6-13 Roppongi, Minato-ku, Tokyo 106; and Serasia Ltd., Asian House, 1 Hennessy Road, Wanchai, Hong Kong.

Printed in Japan.

LCC Card No. 71-162685 ISBN 0-8348-1850-7

CONTENTS

INTRODUCTION

In most maps the city is called Bangkok, and the word in Thai language means the Village of Wild Plums. The Thai people themselves call it by another name: Krungthep, which may be loosely translated as City of Gods, or City of Angels. But it must at once be admitted that this is not the city's complete name. Krungthep, Pramaha Nakorn, Amorn Ratanakosindra, Mahindrayudhya, Mahadilokpop Noparatna Radhani, Buriram, Udom Rajnivet Mahastan, Amorn Pimarn Avatorn Satit, Sakkatutiya Vishnukarm Prasit is Bangkok's royally bestowed title. In English it may be rendered 'city of gods, the great city, the residence of the Emerald Buddha, the impregnable city of the god Indra, the grand capital of the world endowed with nine precious gems, the happy city, abounding in enormous palaces that resemble the heavenly abode where reigns the reincarnated god, a city given by Indra and built by Vishnukarm.'

From this multiplicity of names the last and long-winded one is fortunately reserved for the most august and ceremonial occasions. But the variety of possible names for Bangkok parallels, and also perhaps gives warning of, a more general dilemma in which the visitor finds himself on a first encounter with the city. For Bangkok, to use its most familiar name, is a singularly perplexing city in many ways. It has no readily identifiable center, no single point where one instinctively feels at the heart of things. Rather, it has at least five centers, widely spaced and each serving a distinct purpose. Yet each center seems unrelated to the rest of the city. Within those centers, one gradually perceives, there is a certain plan, even a kind of order. But to the casual visitor this is not at all obvious. The visitor's feeling as he gazes out of the window of a taxi or a tourist bus is one of bewilderment, and sometimes even of dismay.

What he sees is a kaleidoscope of contrasting and usually conflicting images, the one dissolving into the other with apparent nonsensicality: a richly ornamented Buddhist temple, or wat, constructed on some of the most fanciful lines devised by man, and then an anonymous cement and glass office block; a shadowy, boat-clogged canal, or *klong*, swiftly erased by an exhaust-clouded, treeless avenue in the agonies of a vast modern traffic jam; through a briefly opened gate, a glimpse of a cool tropical garden lit with vivid splashes of bougainvillea, and down a narrow alleyway another glimpse of a dim world where naked children play in stagnant pools of oily water; gigantic representations of Doris Day and Rock Hudson beaming down on an early-morning procession of grave young priests in orange robes, carrying brass begging bowls; an unexpected field of rice growing right in the city and, equally surprising, a sleazy row of night clubs and massage parlors with names like Nevada, Las Vegas, California, and Progress. There are yet further incongruities: an elegant, Thai-style restaurant patronized entirely by foreigners; an American-style coffee shop selling hamburgers and Southern fried chicken, crowded with Thai people; traditions jealously guarded here, carelessly abandoned there; a mélange of the exotic and the familiar, East and West, splendid and unspeakable, that stubbornly refuses to form itself into a coherent image. This is Bangkok.

When visitors leave most foreign cities, they take with them a firm impression that, as often as not, is a surprisingly accurate one. Contrary to common belief, quick impressions are frequently more valid than those complicated by long residence and overfamiliarity. Bangkok is an exception to this general rule, at least as far as the Western visitor is concerned. The first impression of it is highly misleading, whether one views the place as a mini-Tokyo in the making or, as the average tourist seems to think, a giant stage set for a production of The King and I. Nor is a second, or even a third impression much more rewarding; for the culture, the climate, the language, and the physical complexity of the place all conspire to thwart real understanding.

All this may partially explain the interesting fact that of all the great cities of Asia, Bangkok is the only one that has never been satisfactorily evoked as a literary background. Tokyo, Singapore, Hong Kong, Peking, Calcutta, have all been used effectively by novelists, and given a fictional reality, but in the surprisingly few novels set in Bangkok, the city has stubbornly refused to come to life. It has been almost equally resistant to travel writers. Of the handful of descriptions that succeed in giving one a feeling of the place, nearly all were written long ago when Bangkok was a much smaller and simpler city than it is today—the impressions, for example, of Conrad when he stopped off as a sailor in the late 19th century, or of Maugham, when he came through on one of his Asian journeys in the twenties.

This is certainly not because modern Bangkok lacks contrast, an element so many writers find essential. Nor does it lack local color, or a complex social fabric, or, despite its relative youth, a sense of history. Bangkok has all these in abundance. Yet it remains elusive. One sees parts of it clearly enough but, somehow, not the whole.

Doubtless there are a number of ways to get closer to the reality of the city, but in any of them the first step must be backward in time. The way in which a city grew reveals much that clarifies the picture it presents today.

PHOTOGRAPH CAPTIONS, PAGES 9–24

9	Fruit vendors at the floating market in Dhonburi
10–11	The Chao Phya River, looking toward Bangkok from the Dhonburi side
12–13	Priests waiting with their begging bowls in the early morning near the Giant Swing
14–15	The new Bangkok: the building in the center is the giant Narai Hotel, its roof crowned by a revolving restaurant
16–17	Thai classical dance: the 'fingernail dance' which originated in the northern part of Thailand
18–19	A girl spinning silk in an area not far from the house of the silk manufacturer James Thompson
20–21	The Dusit Thani Hotel; tallest building in Bangkok. In the center, under scaffolding, a statue of King Rama VI at the entry to Lumpini Park
22–23	Women offering lotus flowers at a temple
24	Giant Buddha at Wat In, visible from a considerable distance

สุวรรณประดิษฐ์

NARAI HOT
Green Spot

A CITY IN THE MAKING

Bangkok is not very old as cities go–and as a capital is even less ancient. Yet to comprehend the Bangkok of today you have to return to its origins. It is also necessary to follow the succession of rulers who comprise the Chakri dynasty, to which the present king belongs, for they were responsible for most of the landmarks of the city.

It was the first Chakri king, known in Thai history as Rama I, who chose the site of the capital in 1782, to symbolize the start of a new era. Until the end of the absolute monarchy in 1932, successive members of the dynasty made the major decisions on expansions and additions that resulted in the city of today.

Bangkok did not simply spring into existence at the whim of the first king, however. Long before the dynasty was born, a place by that name had existed on the site and was well-known to early visitors from the West, who marked it on their rather vague maps of the region. *Bang* in Thai means a village or district, and *kok* is a variety of wild plum that apparently once grew in the area. 'The village of the wild plum' was a small but strategically located fishing village about 25 kilometers from the mouth of the Chao Phya River, the only access by water from the Gulf of Siam to the great capital of Ayudhya upriver. (At one point in geological history the site of Bangkok was actually *on* the Gulf, but over the years silting has steadily made it an inland city) Ayudhya, Thailand's second capital (the first was at Sukhothai, further north) was established in 1350, and over the next 400 years grew into one of Asia's largest and most splendid cities. At its peak, in the late 17th and early 18th centuries, it was more populous than the London of that period, and its art and architecture represented the culminating achievement of the nation's culture–a legacy that was to play a prominent part in the conception and building of the fourth capital at Bangkok. (Dhonburi was, briefly, the third capital.)

During the Ayudhya period, Bangkok remained small in size but its importance increased as the country attracted more and more attention from abroad. Its location, at a wide bend in the river, enabled it more or less to control river traffic up to the capital, and most of the Europeans who came seeking favors from the king stopped at Bangkok until word was sent from Ayudhya advising them whether or not to proceed. One of the Ayudhya kings, Mahachakput (1549–69) raised the status of Bangkok from a village to a town and, at the same time, changed its name to Dhonburi. The new name won little acceptance, either from the residents or from the European visitors, who stubbornly continued to call the place Bangkok. In time, Dhonburi came to mean only the settlement on the other side of the river, a distinction still valid today.

In 1767 there occurred the greatest political, cultural, and psychological catastrophe in Thai history. After a bitter siege that lasted more than two years, Ayudhya fell to the invading Burmese who killed the king and destroyed the entire capital, along with most of its works of art. Of a former population of more than a million, only about 10,000 were left in the ruins. The others were either dead, carried off to Burma as prisoners, or refugees in distant provinces. The once spectacular temples and palaces with their ponds and cool gardens, the thousands of wantonly decapitated images of the Buddha, were left to the ravages of tropical growth for more than a hundred years. Only in the present century, in fact, has a really determined effort been made to clear the jungle and give modern visitors some idea of Ayudhya's former grandeur.

One man who escaped the disaster was a soldier named Taksin who retired to the southeastern province of Chantaburi. A natural leader and a brilliant military tactician, Taksin was able to raise an effective army and recapture the ruined capital within a year of its fall. Shortly after this remarkable achievement, he had himself proclaimed king and embarked on a 15-year reign that consisted largely of repelling further Burmese invasions, recapturing lost Thai territory in the north and northeast, and dealing with numerous palace intrigues.

Ayudhya was too completely destroyed to be rebuilt during such troubled times, and even if King Taksin had had the heart for such a monumental project there was another compelling reason against attempting it. After numerous wars, the enemy knew Ayudhya's approaches too well, and strategic common sense dictated the selection of a new capital. Taksin chose Dhonburi, across the river from Bangkok, and after moving his armies there took the first steps toward turning it into a more permanent city. He rebuilt an old temple, at the site of the present Wat Arun (Temple of Dawn) and, nearby, a fortress-palace that commanded the river approaches. Almost continuous war prevented him from doing much more in the way of building, and today little remains except a few crumbling walls and a memorial statue to the king to remind one of Dhonburi's brief moment on history's stage.

By 1782, the threat of further invasions had diminished, but within the palace at Dhonburi a serious political difficulty had arisen. Possibly as a result of the many strains he had been subjected to, Taksin had begun to behave in a most peculiar manner. There were many in his court who were convinced that he had become insane. The situation became a crisis, there was a palace revolt, and the king was overthrown. Later, in the manner prescribed for royal executions, he was beaten to death on the back of the neck with a sandalwood club.

The popular choice of a successor was another general, Chakri, who had distinguished himself by many victories, the most famous of which had been the capture of Vientiane in present-day Laos. From this victory, he had brought back to Dhonburi one of the greatest treasures of the region, the famous nephrite Buddha image known as Phra Keo, the Emerald Buddha, originally found in northern Thailand in the 15th century. The image had been kept in various northern cities, principally Chiangmai, until 1552, when it had been taken to Vientiane to save it from the Burmese; there it was honored in a special temple, called Wat Phra Keo, until General Chakri brought it back with him.

Chakri was off fighting again, this time in Cambodia, when he heard of the revolt in his capital and hurried back. According to one legend, he marched down what is now called Jetupon Road–the Bangkok road that separates the two sections of Wat Phra Jetupon, or, more commonly, Wat Po–on April 6, 1792. The same day he was offered and accepted the crown, thus inaugurating the new dynasty exactly fifteen years from the day that Ayudhya fell. (Chakri Day is still celebrated on April 6th, and tribute is paid to some of the first king's ashes at Wat Po.)

One of the first decisions of King Rama I (all the Chakri kings were later given the name Rama and numbered according to their rule) was to move the capital across the Chao Phya to Bangkok. In doing so, he was motivated by both strategic and symbolic considerations. From a military standpoint, Bangkok could be defended more easily than Dhonburi, with the river as a natural defense on one side and, on the other, a swampy plain called 'The Sea of Mud,' that extended almost to the gulf. Symbolically, too, a new capital seemed in order, for Dhonburi was associated in the public mind with King Taksin, and Rama I wanted his dynasty to have its own capital.

His plans for it were anything but modest. They called, in fact, for the re-creation of the destroyed Ayudhya, even to the point of duplicating as closely as possible all the well-remembered palaces and temples of the former capital. To this end, an old canal was enlarged and extended to join the bends of the river, forming a sort of artificial island, as had been done at Ayudhya. Those artisans and builders who still remained in the old city were brought down to design and construct the first buildings of the new. Even some of the remaining Ayudhya walls were shipped down the river to be incorporated in the new city.

The most important of these early constructions was the great royal compound to include the King's palace and an elaborate temple for the Emerald Buddha. The riverside site selected by the king for these structures was occupied already by a large number of Chinese

A man wearing amulets to protect him from harm. The price of amulets varies with their potency, and most Thai wear at least one

traders, who were governed by a rich merchant. The merchant and his people agreed to relocate their community in an area a short distance away called Sampeng, which is still the Chinese center of modern Bangkok. Then construction of the temple and palace was begun.

Like the royal palace of Ayudhya, the Bangkok complex occupied exactly one square mile when it was officially described as completed in 1785. Today, it is impossible for a visitor to get more than a faint idea of what it must have looked like then, for regular and drastic alterations and additions have been made over the years, and its setting has completely changed. Of the palace itself, it is probably safe to say that nothing at all of the original remains, with the possible exception of a few buildings in the so-called Inside, where the wives of the king lived. Only Wat Phra Keo, the Temple of the Emerald Buddha, would probably look somewhat familiar to the first ruler, but even that has been constantly restored and altered by subsequent kings. It is perhaps worth noting here that according to Thai Buddhist beliefs, rebuilding earns more merit than restoration or mere preservation. For this reason almost no religious buildings in Bangkok—or, for that matter, elsewhere in Thailand—bear much resemblance to their original appearance. The older structures have been added to, more or less continuously, besides being repainted and refurbished, not invariably with the happiest results.

In the reigns of the early Chakri kings, the Grand Palace enclosure was a complete, self-contained little world—the symbolic center not only of Bangkok but of the kingdom as a whole. The gradual growth of the city has been away from it, but even today, though the king no longer lives there, the Grand Palace and the surrounding area can rightly be described as the ceremonial heart of the capital. The Palace itself, in the old days, consisted of two quite separate sections, known as the Outside and the Inside, terms that adequately describe their functions. The Outside, of which visitors are now permitted to see a small very Westernized part, was used for public audiences and various official and ceremonial occasions. From it the country was governed. The Inside was the king's strictly private domain. Here lived his numerous wives (for the Thai kings of that time, like all other Asian monarchs, were polygamous), their ladies-in-waiting, and their children. No man but the king himself was permitted to enter. The wives rarely ever left the Inside except when on the point of death—it was considered unlucky for anyone to die in the palace—but it was, by all accounts, a pleasant enough place to live. There were flower gardens and fountains and elegant little villas for the wives, who were ranked according to a complex system of seniority that often had more to do with politics than with personal preference. This shut-off part of the palace still exists, still forbidden to all but a select few visitors, and in it until recently, like echoes from the past, a few aged wives of the last king to practice polygamy still lived. They were no longer bound to stay there, of course, but according to a relative of one, they found the silent gardens more congenial than the noisy, modern, and alien city outside.

With the official completion of the palace and Wat Phra Keo in 1785, a grand procession carried the Emerald Buddha across the river to be installed in its new home, a replica of the royal chapel in Ayudhya. There it has remained ever since, its robes changed thrice annually by the king at the beginning of each season, the object of more veneration than any other image in the entire country.

Another of Rama I's contributions to Bangkok was made even before the completion of the palace complex. According to a custom that was probably Brahmanic in origin, a stone pillar was set up to mark the center of the city-to-be, and to provide a home for the capital's guardian spirit who would, it was hoped, protect it from ill fate. At that time in many a Southeast Asian country such a ceremony was accompanied by human sacrifice. The victim preferred was a pregnant woman, who was buried alive beneath the pillar. Naturally there has been some scholarly controversy as to whether Bangkok's pillar

An Indian in the garden of the Grand Palace

Klong scene near a market.
The woman is bringing
melons for sale from the country

conceals a similar grim offering, but current historians are inclined to think not. Sacrifices were occasionally performed in the early Ayudhya period, but had ceased by the time it fell, and what we know of the first king's character makes it unlikely that he would have engaged in such practices.

Today, the pillar, almost unknown to those tourists who complain about the city's lack of a center, is to be found near the Ministry of Defense, across from the Grand Palace compound. Called by the Thai, Lak Muang, it is wooden and nine feet tall, capped with a seven-tiered umbrella, and nearly always well-attended by visitors who come to ask for the spirit's blessings and also to entertain him with performances of Thai music and dancing. Thus far, the pillar has proved to be an effective guardian: in nearly two hundred years Bangkok has never fallen to an enemy, nor has it ever suffered a natural disaster.

Bangkok's cumbrous royal name—"city of gods, the great city, the residence of the Emerald Buddha, etc., etc.," was bestowed somewhat prematurely by the king in 1786. At this time, the only feature that justified the resounding title was the Grand Palace complex, and Bangkok consisted mostly of the Chinese trading community, some floating Thai houses along the river, and a few Buddhist temples dating back to the Ayudhya period. It was surrounded by a medieval wall with 63 gates, which was 9 feet thick and 12 feet tall, to protect the city from attack. Rama I quickly embarked on an ambitious building program, however, and numbers of the city's landmarks today owe their origins, if not their present appearance, to projects conceived by him.

The capital's largest temple, Wat Po, constructed on the site of an older wat, dates from this reign. Adjacent to the palace, it took seven years to build and became a favorite with Chakri kings, perhaps because of the legend of General Chakri's famous march down Jetupon Road which divides the temple complex from the monk's quarters. Most of the succeeding members of the dynasty made extensive additions to it. Another important temple, less familiar to modern visitors, was Wat Sutat, which has extraordinarily fine carved doors and windows, and some beautiful murals.

Bangkok was planned, as Ayudhya had been, principally in terms of transportation by water. To this end, Rama I built a large number of *klong*s to facilitate communication in the expanding city. Several of these canals were specifically made wide enough for boat races, a spectacle which had been a popular diversion in the old capital and one which, obviously, the new one had to have as well. It was not until the reign of the fourth king, some sixty years later, that Bangkok acquired roads worthy of the name. Until then, the river and canals served as streets for the bulk of the population, a characteristic that resulted, inevitably, in the city's being described by most of its early European visitors as 'the Venice of the East.' Horse-drawn vehicles, and later the automobile, signalled the end of most of the *klongs*, and for a visitor today it is hard to realize that even twenty-five or thirty years ago most of the major avenues of the city were mere tracks bordered on either side by far more populous waterways.

Annually, at the end of the rainy season, which also marked the end of the Buddhist Lent period, the kings of Ayudhya had embarked on a splendid merit-acquiring procession called a *kathin*, in which they presented gifts to the priests of several temples. For his own *kathin*s, Rama I had built a fantastic collection of carved and gilded barges to transport him and his vast retinue to the wats (mainly Wat Arun) along the river on this important occasion. This procession became one of the highlights of the Bangkok ceremonial year, with crowds of people flocking to the riverside to watch the glittering barges rowed by men in scarlet who chanted rhythmically as they pulled the oars. The king sat on a high throne on the largest barge, the prow of which formed the arching neck and head of a mythical swan. Following the revolution of 1932, when the absolute monarchy came to an end, the king lived abroad for a period of almost fifteen years and the

The new Indra Hotel under construction.
Children playing on New Road, one
of the city's oldest streets
now being widened and equipped with sewers

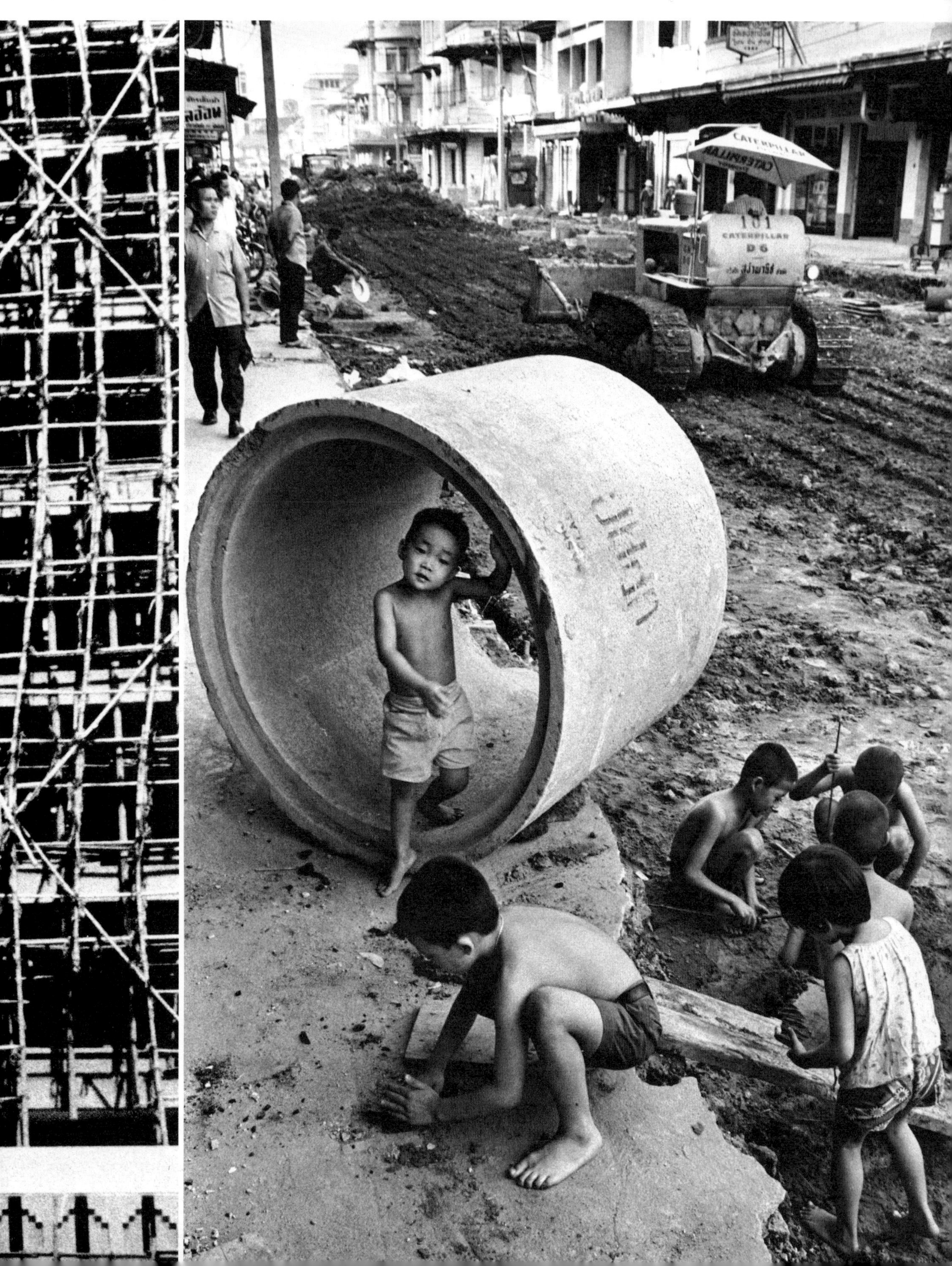
CATERPILLAR
101
CATERPILLAR
D 6

View from the Golden Mount,
once the highest
point in the city

splendid boats fell into disrepair in their shelters on the Dhonburi side of the river. In the late fifties the government decided to revive the procession and it has once again taken its place among the major spectacles of Asia.

The founder of Bangkok died in 1809, at the age of 72, after a reign of twenty-eight eventful years. Even in death he added yet another tradition to the capital, for he was cremated in the great oval field outside the palace and the field became established as the site of royal funerals. The place is known as the Phramane Ground (*phra mane* are the Thai words for royal crematorium). Sometimes the name is given simply as Sanam Luang (the King's field), and all subsequent kings and high-ranking people have been cremated there. In Buddhist countries, however, death is not the gloomy affair it is in the West—particularly not the death of a venerable person who has spent a lifetime earning merit by temple building and other good deeds—and the Phramane Ground has never acquired a funereal atmosphere, for all the royal ashes it has seen. It is, in fact, one of the most lively places in the city, the site of the colourful weekend market every Saturday and Sunday and, on other days, a popular meeting place for bicycle riders, footballers, kite flyers, medicine men, and for people out for a stroll.

King Rama II continued his father's building projects and began more of his own, branching out from the classical Ayudhya style of building to include some in Chinese and even European styles, for by this time more and more Westerners were turning up in the young capital. The much-admired and much-photographed *prang*, or tower, on Wat Arun (near the remains of King Taksin's fortress-palace in Dhonburi) was one of this king's conceptions, and he had it decorated with thousands of bits of broken porcelain so that from a distance it seems covered with flowers.

The second reign was also a period of considerable development in the art of Thai dancing, and the king himself supervised many changes in the classic forms that date back to the Sukothai period. The Thai formal dance (as opposed to the very informal folk dances) consists of a number of different types, each with its own particular function. But generally speaking there are two prominent classifications: dances to be performed inside the palace, for the king's own pleasure, and those to be presented outside. In the former, because of the ban on males in the palace interior, only girls took part, and the costumes were elaborately bejewelled. The latter were either all-male or mixed, and the dress was less spectacular. The dances enjoyed by so many visitors today are often a mixture of the two, though female dancers still predominate. Often they take male roles, with one notable exception—the role of Hanuman, the white monkey. Hanuman is one of the key characters in the Ramayana legend from which most of the dances derive, and is almost always danced by a man. Indeed, numerous dancers have built careers on their interpretation of it.

The third Chakri king, Rama III (1824–51), has been largely ignored by both Western and Thai historians, who have tended to concentrate on the far more spectacular reigns of the two kings who followed him. Yet, though outwardly traditional, Rama III was responsible for many significant developments in the country as a whole as well as in Bangkok. It is probably safe to say that the revolutionary developments of the succeeding reigns would have been impossible had he not provided the groundwork.

Like the kings before him, he was an enthusiastic builder, concerned with practical as well as spiritual undertakings. He built numerous new canals (one of which was 30 miles long) to make travel easier between Bangkok and the countryside. He also built nine new temples and made additions and repairs to more than 60 others including both Wat Po and Wat Phra Keo. By the time he came to the throne, Bangkok was firmly established as the cultural center of the country, and the best provincial artists were flocking to it, contributing their handiwork to already existing palaces and temples as well as to the king's new architectural projects. One result of this was the massive reclining Buddha at Wat Po, a figure 90 feet long, made of brick and mortar and covered with gold. The feet of the image, inlaid with delicate designs in mother-of-pearl, bear testimony to the high standards of artistic workmanship during the reign, as do the murals on the walls of the building that houses the image.

Rama III was a keen advocate of public education, and this was revealed in two unique projects. One was the effort to turn Wat Po into a kind of bookless library for the benefit of those of his subjects who wished to partake of the available knowledge of the time. He did this by having murals painted, dealing with such subjects as war, religion, medicine, astrology, botany, geography, and history, and by having the columns of several buildings inscribed with various herbal medicine remedies. Anyone who wanted could thus receive a reasonably liberal education simply by strolling about the temple compound. Even today, the temple is the center of Thai herbal medicine lore, with experts who come to lecture on their specialities and buy and sell certain rare ingredients.

The other project was rather more whimsical. Noting the Western ships that were calling at Bangkok with increasing regularity, the king came to the conclusion that the old Chinese junk, which had contributed so much to Thai economy, was likely soon to become obsolete. The prospect of future generations being unable to recall this once-mighty vessel disturbed him. Accordingly, when he decided to add a building to Wat Yanawa in the Chinese district of Bangkok, he departed drastically from tradition and had it built in the shape of a junk. This fanciful structure exists today, though in a somewhat dilapidated condition, and possibly still instructs some of the young generation who, as the king foresaw, have never seen a real floating junk.

The first purely European-style buildings appeared in Bangkok during this reign, and the first Europeans took up semipermanent residence in the capital. Some of these were missionaries, who were to exert a strong influence over the next king. Others were businessmen, among them an Englishman named Robert Hunter, who lived in a floating house on the river. Thanks to one of his visitors, we are offered a glimpse of what it was like for a foreigner to live in Bangkok in those days. Mr. Hunter's guest kept a diary, in which he wrote an account of a day during his visit:

> "We breakfasted at 10 and after that meal were wont to walk backwards and forwards on the splendid balcony Mr. Hunter had erected, as much for exercise as to enjoy an uninterrupted half hour's chat. Then Mr. Hunter betook himself to the counting house. . . . Occasionally we amused ourselves at Mr. Hunter's by playing LaGrace, and we were once or twice guilty of a game at ringtaw. Night, however, brought with it its enlivening candle-lights. The darker and more stormy the nights the more brilliantly illuminated the rooms used to be, and if the weather was particularly damp, we made ourselves comfortable with a good dinner and some fine old sherry, and then as a wind-up a drop of hot whisky toddy. . . . One hour before midnight, as indicated by the old clock at Mr. Hunter's house, was the signal for us to disperse for the night, and long before that time arrived, the whole city was hushed in deep repose."

Another visitor during Rama III's reign was the French Monseigneur Pallegoix, who left an enthusiastic description of Bangkok at that time:

> "It is situated on the two banks of the Me-Nam, eight leagues from the sea. In reality the city forms an island two leagues in cirumference; it is surrounded by castellated ramparts and flanked by towers or bastions from one end to the other. Situated in the midst of boundless gardens consisting of luxuriant year-round growth, Bangkok makes a very picturesque sight; ships and a multitude of flag-bedecked junks cluster in rows at the edges of the two banks; golden spires, cupolas, and beautifully constructed lofty pyramids, embellished with designs of multi-colored por-

Selling lottery tickets on New Road.
To win is the dream of many a
Thai, and the day before the
draw finds temples crowded with people
praying for luck

celain which soar into the air. The tiered roofs of the pagodas, ornamented with gold and covered with varnished tile, glitter as they reflect the rays of the sun. Thousands of shops floating in two rows are spread out before you, following the curved structure of a majestic river crossed in every direction by thousands of crafts, most of which are very elegant. The fort, white as snow, the city with its towers and numerous gates, the straight canals which run through the city, the golden spire at the palace seen from all four sides, the variety of buildings in Indian, Chinese, and European styles, the peculiar costumes of different nationalities, the sound of musical instruments, the singing in the playhouses, the movement and the life which ornates this great city; all these things present the foreigner with delightful and surprising spectacle."

Monseigneur Pallegoix made the mistake of many foreigners of confusing the Thai word *menam,* which means 'river, with the name of the river that flows through the capital. But otherwise his description must be an accurate view of the place in 1830. Of the 'castellated ramparts' he saw—part of Rama I's medieval wall—only one small segment remains today on Phra Sumain Road.

Of all the kings of Thailand, the one best known to the average Westerner is Rama IV, also known as King Mongkut, who reigned from 1851 to 1868. This is not, however, because of his many remarkable qualities as a person, or because he was the leader who set his nation on the road to becoming a modern state. His fame abroad rests almost solely, and most unfortunately, on the largely fictional portrait of him in the musical comedy *The King and I*. This in turn owed its existence (and many of its mistakes) to the romantic memoirs of a nineteenth-century Englishwoman named Anna Leonowens, who was engaged by the king to teach some of his children. Thai people are grieved by this injustice, for it has resulted in a widely held belief that Rama IV was a semibarbarian who kept a harem and learned the rudiments of civilized behavior from a schoolmarm. In truth, at the time he was offered the throne he was the abbot of a Buddhist monastery in Bangkok, had been a priest for 27 of his 47 years, and was already keenly aware of Western advances in science and technology through his long-standing friendships with a number of American missionaries, as well as from a large correspondence with friends abroad. It was simply an indication of his modern turn of mind that he broke with tradition and took on a European to instruct the crown prince—something no previous Thai king would have dreamed of doing. True, he acquired 35 wives after becoming king, and by them had 82 children; but this was not extraordinary in the Asia of that period, and the harem that so shocked (and intrigued) Anna and her readers served more of a political than a romantic purpose.

Rama IV is the first of the Chakri kings of whom we have a really clear picture, not only through the photographs taken of him, but through his own English correspondence and the numerous impressions of him by Western visitors other than Anna. Examining these sources, it is easy to see why, after his son King Chulalongkorn, he is the most admired of all the kings by present-day Thai. He had a variety of interests that ranged from archaeology to astronomy and, considering the time and place, a remarkable tolerance. He gave full freedom to foreign missionaries to operate in the kingdom, wisely foreseeing that their educational contributions would probably be greater than the number of their conversions (as, indeed, proved to be the case). He was also aware of, and interested in, the activities of the world beyond. When he heard of the American Civil War, he dispatched a letter offering Thai war elephants to President Lincoln, an offer that was regretfully turned down due to the problems of transportation and the unsuitable climatic conditions in North America.

Mongkut's effect on Bangkok was considerable. It was during his reign that Bangkok changed from a remote Oriental capital, known principally for its temples and palaces, into a thriving center of international commerce where foreign faces (and foreign ways) were no longer rarities. Sir John Bowring, who negotiated an important treaty between Thailand and Great Britain, visited the city in 1855, noting that "all that remained to represent foreign trade was one English (half-caste) merchant, one Armenian, and a few Anglo-Indians from Bombay and Surat." But only two years later, as a result of a number of similar treaties with other Western countries and the active encouragement of the king, 200 foreign ships called at Bangkok, and foreign embassies and trading companies were being established there.

Since transportation was still mainly by water, most of the foreigners built their establishments on or near the river, the majority in the vicinity of the present-day Oriental Hotel. The present French and Portuguese embassies date from this period; the British embassy was originally located where the General Post Office now stands, and only moved to its new site shortly before the second World War. This area remained the center of 'European Bangkok' for nearly a hundred years, and only recently has the foreign community shifted its base to the section along the Sukumwit Road known as Bangkapi. In Rama IV's day, and for a very long time afterward, Bangkapi was a tranquil rural region of canals and rice fields.

It was largely because of this concentration of Europeans that Bangkok got its first real Western-style street. According to Prince Chula Chakrabongse, who wrote a history of the Chakri dynasty, "Western people had been accustomed for their health to take the air of an evening riding in horse-drawn carriages, and owing to the lack of suitable roads in Bangkok, they were suffering from bad health and illnesses. The king said he was grateful for their complaints, and added that he felt ashamed of the dirt and filth of the narrow lanes of Bangkok, and he began a road- and bridge-building programme."

A number of good roads resulted, including Charoen Krung Road, which was laid in 1862 and which, as the New Road of Western visitors, quickly became the best-known street in the city. Running parallel to the river in the area of the embassies, it satisfied their need for a place 'to take the air of an evening,' and was soon lined with shops and trading companies, a few of which may still be seen today among and behind the buildings of recent years.

In temple building and reconstruction, Rama IV was as enthusiastic as his predecessors, though many of his projects were outside Bangkok, for he had a keen interest in the country's ancient capitals as well as in its modern one. He made frequent trips to Sukhothai, Ayudhya, and Lopburi. In Nakorn Prathom, south of Bangkok, he restored the great pagoda, the largest in Thailand and today a popular site with tourists and Buddhist pilgrims. In Bangkok itself, he added his own touch to Wat Po, a temple which, as we have seen, was a favorite of the Chakri kings. Just west of the main chapel in the compound can be seen four large *chedi*s, or pagodas, each in a different color of glazed tile. The green one was contributed by Rama I to hold a mutilated Buddha image brought from Ayudhya. The white and yellow *chedi*s were built by Rama III, the first to commemorate his father's reign, the second as a memorial to his own. Rama IV ordered the blue *chedi* to be built for his reign and then, in a characteristic gesture, commanded that all four should be enclosed so that no others could be added. It was only proper that the first four Chakri kings should have memorials close together, he noted, since they had all known one another personally; but if the following kings of the dynasty felt obliged to follow the practice, the temple compound would become overcrowded with *chedi*s; and besides, the significance of the first four would be lost.

Rama IV should also perhaps be given credit for another of Bangkok's outstanding sights, the Golden Mount, though it was actually the second king who first conceived of the idea of enhancing the flat city with a man-made mountain. The effort was not a success, however, for the mass of mortar and rocks soon began to crack and sink into the marshy earth. It was Rama IV who returned to this

Street near Pratunam Market, a
popular shopping area.
Traffic jams are commonplace in Bangkok

K LINE

A peaceful *klong* in the center of the city

Fruit vendors at the Weekend Market. *Right,* unloading coconuts on the riverbank. In the background is Wat Arun under scaffolding for repair

ambitious project and applied modern engineering techniques that resulted, in the next reign, in the striking 'mountain' topped by a golden spire that contains a relic of the Buddha. For many years, until the post-war advent of tall buildings, the Golden Mount was the only place that offered a really panoramic view of the capital. While that distinction is now gone, it is still the center of one of the Bangkok year's most festive fairs, during which hundreds of visitors climb its winding steps with lighted torches.

It was during the reign of Rama IV, too, that a curious, now unfortunately defunct Brahmin ceremony first came to the attention of the court and was established as a popular annual ritual. This was known as the Swinging Ceremony. It was held in January and was one of the ways devised to entertain the supreme Brahmin deity Phra Isuan, who was believed to visit the earth for a ten-day stay every year and had to be suitably honored and amused. To judge from old accounts (the ceremony was discontinued late in the reign of Rama VII) the Swinging Ceremony was obviously a very elaborate entertainment, with a procession of several thousand people bearing an image of the god to Sao Chingcha (Giant Swing Square) across from Wat Suthat. Three teams of four young men each did the actual swinging, sitting cross-legged on the swing seat which was suspended from a crossbar some seventy feet high. They set the swing in motion with coordinated movements, and when it had reached a perilous arc of about 90 degrees, slowly stood up. The object of the spectacle, apart from amusing the god, was to claim a container of money attached to a bamboo pole equal in height to the swing's crossbar. To snatch it, the swing's arc had to attain 180 degrees. To make the whole event a little more stimulating and difficult, the young man who plucked the money from the pole was supposed to do so with his teeth.

The impressive red swing that now stands on the site is not the one used in Rama VI's reign, but it does have a rather indirect connection with that remarkable ruler. It was erected in 1919 by the Louis T. Leonowens Company in memory of the firm's founder, who had come to Thailand as a child with his mother, the legendary Anna, and later returned as a businessman.

By the time King Mongkut died in 1868 of a fever contracted while viewing a solar eclipse at an observatory he had built in the south, his building program for Bangkok has resulted in new roads, bridges, and canals, as well as in an expansion of the city boundaries that carried it far beyond its modest original limits. It remained for his son, King Chulalongkorn, to carry on and vastly enlarge the program and to become, during his 42-year reign, by far the greatest of all the royal influences on the city's development.

King Rama V, or Chulalongkorn as he is known to most Thai today, demonstrated what sort of ruler he was going to be on his coronation day. Among the rules of etiquette governing an audience with the king was one requiring visitors to prostrate themselves on the floor in the royal presence—a rule that had been criticized by a number of foreigners, including Anna. Chulalongkorn ordered those who came on that first day to pay him homage, to rise, saying that henceforth no one need crawl before the king.

It was a dramatic gesture, and a symbolic one; for he soon proved that he would not be hampered by tradition in the vital task of modernizing his country. He was the first king to travel abroad and see for himself what was going on in other countries. He came back with a vast assortment of new ideas about how a kingdom should be governed in general and, in particular, of how a national capital should look. He abolished slavery which, in a mild form, had been practiced in the country for centuries. He brought in foreign advisors to assist in the reorganization of the government departments, and in the building of railways to link remote provinces with Bangkok. During his reign Bangkok changed drastically in appearance, so that by the time of his death in 1910 almost all the best-known monuments and features of the present-day city had been built, and many of its

Children enjoy swimming
in the Chao Phya River toward
the end of the day

future developments were clearly indicated in his intentions.

A few of those undertakings suggest the breadth of his contribution. On his first trip to Europe, impressed by the broad avenues of Paris and Berlin, he decided that Bangkok should have one of comparable proportions. The result was Rajadamnern Avenue (Royal Progress Avenue), which runs some five kilometers from the Phramane Ground to the National Assembly Hall. It was the king's hope that this grand avenue would become the fashionable shopping center of Bangkok, in the manner of its counterparts in other capitals. But in this the city has shown its peculiar stubbornness where deliberate planning is involved. The smart shops, when they finally came, chose the other side of the city in a section that King Chulalongkorn would have looked upon as countryside, leaving Rajadamnern to various government offices and to the military, through whose center it passes. On ceremonial occasions such as the king's birthday or a visit from distinguished foreign visitors, it is brilliantly illuminated and, by night, is at least an approximation to what Rama V hoped it would be. But by day, especially at weekends when offices are closed, it is rather deserted, with inadequate trees and undistinguished architecture.

Road building in general enjoyed a boom during Rama V's reign, and by the closing years of the century more of the city's commerce was being transacted by land than by water. In 1871, a wealthy Chinese resident presented the first rickshaw to the king, and within a single generation this form of transportation had proved so popular that the government was compelled in 1901 to pass a law limiting the number of rickshaws in the interest of public safety. In 1888, horsedrawn trams appeared, later to be electrified and to continue to operate in the city until a few years ago, when they finally admitted defeat by the motor bus. The rickshaws themselves gave way in time to pedicabs, which in turn were replaced by motorized versions of the same thing. These are still operating, but their days, too, are clearly numbered. In 1902, one of the king's sons drove the first automobile along a Bangkok street; by 1908, there were over 300 cars in the city, and the roads were rapidly being improved to meet their demands.

There were still, however, numerous canals in 'the Venice of the East,' and bridging them was one of the king's particular enthusiasms. He established a tradition of presenting a new bridge to the city every year on his birthday, and many of Bangkok's handsomest bridges, particularly in the area around Rajadamnern Avenue, owe their existence to this custom.

In architecture, the king's tastes were considerably less traditional than those of his predecessors, again revealing his eagerness to learn from foreign models. Though appreciative of classic Thai styles, he found European innovations more suited to modern life and government. Thus nearly all the palaces and public buildings built in his reign were wholly or partly Western in design. The National Assembly Hall was built by Italian engineers, using marble from their native country. Dusit Palace, which the king built as a retreat from the ceremonial formalities of the Grand Palace, is also in Western style. Even in the Grand Palace itself he added a purely European annex for the reception of foreign guests. His powerful influence in such matters resulted in a popular passion for Victorian architecture, the leading style of the day, and some of his children and relatives built palaces that may still be considered masterpieces of this unjustly maligned art form. Most of these palaces passed out of royal hands following the revolution of 1932, and many of them have been destroyed by what is generally referred to as progress. But the connoisseur who prowls the streets of the Dusit area will be rewarded by many unexpected beauties.

One, which actually belongs to the following reign, is Phya Thai Palace, built by King Rama VI. Today Phya Thai Palace is the Phra Mongkut Army Hospital, and is not on any tourist itinerary. Yet a visitor will find more than a suggestion of its former splendor if he wanders through its spacious, now sadly neglected gardens. There is

On Klong Rangsit, just outside the city and near the airport. The large water jars come from southern Thailand by boat

a marvelous crystal-palace pavilion (now a canteen for doctors and nurses) where gala dances used to be held, with some superbly useless turrets and gingerbread on the main building. Behind it is a totally unexpected little Greek temple with a pool that is now dry. For a brief period in the late twenties, after Rama VI's death, Phya Thai Palace was Bangkok's most luxurious hotel, and performances of Thai classical dance were given in the Greek temple—a juxtaposition of cultures that, to judge from photographs, was quite enchanting.

Even in Buddhist temple building, the principal method of gaining religious merit, King Rama V was no traditionalist. Perhaps the most celebrated temple to rise in his reign, Wat Benchamabophit (which means the Temple of the Fifth King, and is known to tourists as the Marble Temple), was designed by a royal prince who used Italian marble from Carrara and departed in numerous other ways from the conventional style, including the use of stained-glass windows inspired by the cathedrals of Europe. Among the many interesting features of this beautiful temple compound is a small building near the monks' quarters, which the king used when he spent the obligatory period in the priesthood required of all devout young Thai men. Formerly situated in the Grand Palace enclosure, it was moved to the Marble Temple after his death. The interior walls are decorated with charming murals depicting scenes from his early life, including the first trip the king made outside Thailand, to Penang and Indonesia. Also in Wat Benchamabophit is a unique collection of Buddha images, displayed in the gallery surrounding the courtyard of the main chapel, and representing all periods and styles of Thai Buddhist art as well as several from foreign countries.

A final significant development during the reign of Rama V was the steady expansion of the city away from the old area immediately around the original palace. Partly this was due to the simple fact that the old area was becoming too congested. A glance at the city map today will show that the majority of its temples are located within a relatively small area, mostly in the 'island' formed by the bend in the river. But it was also due to the king's desire to escape, now and then, to what was in his time the suburbs; for he was subjected to pressures greater than those of any previous Chakri ruler. Apart from supervising the wide-scale modernization of the country, it was he who steered the delicate diplomatic course that saved Thailand from colonization by one of the European powers—a task whose difficulty is suggested by the fact that Thailand was the only country in Southeast Asia to remain independent. Increasingly, the king found his ceremonial duties burdensome, and for a change of pace he repaired to various palaces in the area now known as Dusit. The court, of course, followed, and Dusit soon became a fashionable residential district. This is true even today, for the present king has his residence at Chitlada Palace, across from Wat Benchamabophit, and uses the old Grand Palace only for the most formal occasions.

Another of the fifth king's favorite retreats that is seen by many visitors today is Bang Pa-In Palace, on an island in the Chao Phya River just below Ayudhya. There is a fairy-tale charm about this summer palace which includes an elaborately decorated Chinese building presented to the king by a group of Bangkok businessmen, and also an elegant little Thai-style pavilion that is probably the most photographed single structure in all the country. (Models of the pavilion have been the main feature of Thailand's contribution to several world's fairs.) Also at Bang Pa-In, there is a touching monument with inscriptions in both Thai and English, erected by King Chulalongkorn in memory of one of his favorite wives who was drowned in a boating accident near the island.

King Chulalongkorn's death in 1910 marked the end of an era in Thailand as surely as Queen Victoria's did in England. During his reign, the longest of any Chakri monarch thus far, the country had changed in countless ways. Nowhere was this more apparent than in the capital. Bangkok had become one of the largest and most important cities in Southeast Asia, with a cosmopolitan population and a metropolitan momentum that no longer depended on royal encouragement for its growth. Subsequent kings could, and did, leave their mark on the city. Chulalongkorn's son, Rama VI, for example, transformed the Royal Pages' School into the country's first university, which he named after his father; but what might be called old Bangkok was firmly established by the second decade of the present century.

Nor has that part of the capital really changed very much in the intervening years. Photography came to Thailand along with many other innovations in Rama V's years, so there is a record of what Bangkok was like sixty years ago. Looking through these old pictures, what surprises is how many of them appear to have been taken only recently. Some of the street scenes around Wat Suthat could be contemporary.

The part of Bangkok where the most dramatic changes have taken place lies on the other side of the city, and some of these changes, it is safe to say, would have surprised even the farsighted Rama V.

Booming new Bangkok, which comes as such a shock to many visitors conditioned by romantic pictures of the old, is actually of very recent origin—not very much more than ten or fifteen years old. The long period from King Chulalongkorn's death to the end of the Second World War saw little change in the city, undoubtedly because of the social and economic upheaval brought about by the 1932 revolution which ended the absolute monarchy, and because of the world depression of those years. Somerset Maugham passed through in the late twenties, and while he was as impressed as any tourist with the temples and palaces, the rest of the city failed to rouse him. New Road he described as hot and dusty, its merchandise fly-spotted and uninteresting. The commercial side of Bangkok he found indistinguishable from that of any other large Oriental city he knew.

During the war, a strongly nationalistic sentiment resulted in a number of buildings that combined classic Thai features (especially in roof decoration) with Western architecture, and also in the Victory Monument, which commemorates a victory during the brief Indo-China war of 1941. After the war another period of political instability set in, and for about ten years the changes in the city were slight. Perhaps the most significant, in view of what was about to come, was the gradual relocation of more and more embassies, shops, and hotels out in the direction of the Sukumwit Highway which, even after the war, was a narrow road bordered on either side by *klongs*. Just prior to the war, the British Embassy had been one of the first to move to this decidedly suburban district; and after the end of hostilities the Americans followed, moving to Wireless Road. But perhaps the biggest single incentive to development in the area was the decision of the government, in the early fifties, to locate the new Erawan Hotel there.

The real boom started in the second half of the fifties and shows no sign of stopping even now. In those years nearly as many new buildings were added to Bangkok as in the first two hundred years of its history. Most of them, moreover, are radically different in design and function from anything in the city's past—apartment blocks, hotels, shopping centers, bowling alleys, offices, cinemas, night clubs—transforming the new Bangkok to such an extent that an old-timer returning after an absence of, say, fifteen years might find it impossible to get his bearings in the Sukumwit area. The road itself is now a noisy, six-lane avenue that fullfils in popularity, if not in grandeur, King Chulalongkorn's dreams for Rajadamnern. From only a few hundred first-class hotel rooms available in the city in 1950, the city's total has risen to more than 6,000, a sizeable proportion of them either on or near Sukumwit. In the fifties, Bangkok could boast of only a single example of that American phenomenon, the shopping center; today there are dozens, and still more under construction. Silom Road, once a tranquil, predominantly residential area, is lined with glassy, air-conditioned office buildings. The New Petchburi Road, which didn't even exist fifteen years ago, has become a major traffic artery by day and by night, a garish strip of cheap night clubs and massage parlors that for sheer iniquity possibly surpass anything to be found elsewhere in modern Asia.

The old cliché 'the Venice of the East' can certainly no longer be applied to the new Bangkok. Once every small lane, or *soi*, had its own *klong*, which served an urgent sanitary need, and the *klongs* along the larger streets were navigable. Today, most of these have either become extra lanes for congested streets, or have been covered by new buildings. The only major canal left in the area of the building boom is the one behind the British Embassy which, ironically, is now being favorably regarded as a possible answer to the seemingly insoluble problem of traveling by land to and from outlying residential districts.

And the city is still growing. It now claims a population of close to three million—a necessarily rough estimate, and probably a conservative one in view of the steady flow of people from the provinces to the capital. Plans were recently announced to expand Bangkok to hold more than twice that number within the next twenty-five years, and local experts believe it will extend all the way to the Gulf of Thailand by the year 2000. It also seems inevitable that more and more of the population will move across the river to Dhonburi where land is cheaper and the pace still a bit slower. Already, commuting is an established part of Bangkok life, with many workers taking more than an hour to get to their offices each morning.

Along with all this sudden prosperity and expansion have come the inevitable metropolitan problems so familiar to city-dwellers in the West, problems largely unknown in the Bangkok of only two decades ago. Slums have grown like ugly abscesses. Crime has increased at a startling rate, especially murder and theft. Juvenile delinquency, a totally new phenomenon, is a common topic of discussion at any gathering of older residents. Traffic jams have made the rush hour a nightmare and increasing air pollution demands urgent attention. More and more of the city's population is suffering from nervous tension brought on by all the competition and cultural confusion.

It is all too easy to take a single one of the aspects of present-day Bangkok and call it the whole. This is what the average visitor is inclined to do, seeing Bangkok either as a terrifying example of Westernization run amok, or as a travel-article place full of extravagant temples and smiling people, or as both co-existing uneasily in a single city. Both are parts of the city, and perhaps the most strikingly visible to a newcomer; but they remain *only* parts to natives of the place, the great majority of whom live in worlds only incidentally concerned with the two extremes. Possibly the best way to gain some understanding of the city as it is today, is to examine each of its separate worlds and their distinguishing features. Some of them are as obvious as the glittering spire of the Golden Mount; others are so hidden that they go unnoticed by most visitors and even many residents; all of them in combination make the city what it is.

THE MANY WORLDS OF BANGKOK

THE TOURIST WORLD

A stone Chinese guardian figure at Wat Arun
one of many brought back as ballast
in empty rice boats
returning from trade in China in
the 19th century

Girls in a massage parlor
wait for the customers to select
the ones they would like
through one-way glass windows

One of the girls from a massage parlor on New Petchburi Road takes a breath of air. The bicycle carries a selection of traditional Thai sweets

A giant bronze Buddha head of the Sukothai period (12th–13th c.) in the National Museum

Nineteenth-century Chinese carvings of Europeans decorating Wat Rajpradit (*left, right*), and Wat Po, *center*

The Temple of the Emerald Buddha
(Wat Phra Keo), the
most sacred of Bangkok's shrines

A Chinese figure at Wat Po and, *right,* part of the gigantic Reclining Buddha, the principal attraction of the temple. Wat Po dates from the very beginning of the city of Bangkok

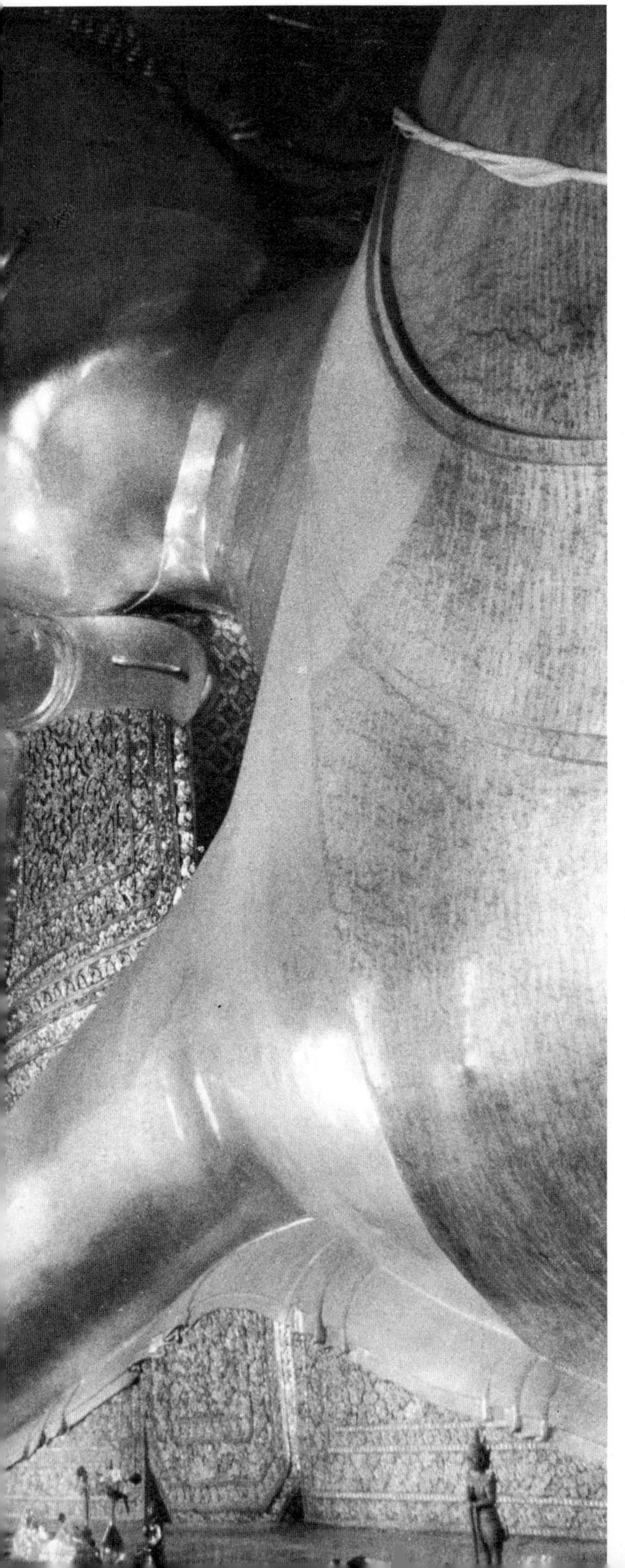

According to a survey made not long ago, the average tourist who comes to Bangkok is middle-aged, reasonably well-to-do, and values comfort more than local color. Whether this view is accurate or not, is hard to decide. It may perhaps be locally colored by the fact that comfort is what tourists certainly find in the city–apart from the strange and fascinating sights that are grouped together under the heading of local color. Tourism is now one of Thailand's major industries, accounting for 29 million US dollars in revenue in 1966, and increasing year by year. Bangkok itself probably produces the lion's share of this revenue since almost all tourists spend some time there, while rather few go very far out of the capital.

The city is easily reached by air, land, and even by sea. Surprisingly enough, in this age of air travel, a large number of tourists came until recently by sea in the cruise ships that dock at the mouth of the river each spring on their way to the cherry blossoms of Japan. Rather few people came by land—for this entails a long train journey from Malaysia. And in the last decade the jet has virtually effaced all other ways of getting to Bangkok. The jet has made of the city one of the three major travel destinations in Asia (the other two being Tokyo and Hong Kong), and most visitors touch Thai soil first at Don Muang airport. 200,000 of them arrive every year. Bangkok is prepared for the influx. All the international chains have built hotels in Bangkok of recent years, and there are the government-owned Erawan, and the historic but refurbished Oriental. Besides these, what seems like a forest of others have sprung up, and are still visibly springing up in the central districts.

The average tourist, according to the same survey, is likely to stay in Bangkok for three to five days, and during that time he divides his excursions between sightseeing and shopping—with emphasis on the former. Tourism is big business these days, but even now the day of independent guides is not quite past. A few are still to be found at many of the major temples in the city, ready to assist that rare but still not extinct breed, the independent tourist who prefers not to see his temples table d'hôte but to pick and choose à la carte.

But most tourists now come in groups, their sightseeing arranged and streamlined by one or other of the numerous travel agencies whose guides are mostly licensed. Many of these guides are graduates of the Guide Training Course conducted by the Tourist Organization of Thailand and the Chulalongkorn University, and have passed examinations in history and art, in English, and even in Thai customs.

It is a strange, highly selective view of Bangkok and Thai culture that the tourist gets from a visit to the capital. The three standard day tours of the city take him, for the most part, to a very few temples—Wat Po, Wat Benchamabophit, sometimes Wat Suthat, the Grand Palace, the Wat Phra Keo complex. Then there is the early morning trip to the Floating Market across the river in Dhonburi, including a visit to the Royal Barges and a tour of Wat Arun. The Floating Market trip started long ago as an admirable attempt to give visitors a glimpse of 'ordinary Thai life,' though it is debatable how ordinary that life ever was in terms of what the ordinary Bangkok resident experienced. Latterly, relentless and doubtless inevitable commercialism has dimmed whatever authenticity and charm the Floating Market had. What the tourist now sees is a cunningly contrived simulacrum of Thai life aimed precisely at *him*. In terms of actual Thai life it is about as authentic as another popular enterprise included in many tourist itineraries and known as Timland (TIM—Thailand in Miniature), a Disneyland-inspired creation where everything from elephants to folk dancing is presented with surprisingly effective professionalism. Authentic or not, however, most visitors manfully get out of bed at dawn and see the Floating Market. No doubt the majority come away convinced that the average Thai lives in a picturesque floating house and buys his provisions from a pretty girl in a boat laden with exotic fruits and vegetables.

Other places are included on some schedules. Many tourists visit the National Museum, the largest collection of its kind in Southeast

A dancer in the elaborate costume of Thai classical dance. *Right,* another dancer performing in honor of the spirit at Lak Muang, the pillar marking the 'center' of Bangkok

Asia, partly housed in an old palace dating back to Rama III, adjacent to Thammasat University, and partly in a gleaming modern building completed only a few years ago. Some, too, go to see two private collections of Asian art that are open to the public on certain days. One of these is at Suan Pakkard, on Sri Ayudhya Road—a palace belonging to Princess Chumbhot of Nakorn Sawan—which has a beautiful garden as well as a rare lacquer pavilion brought down from Ayudhya. Another is the American Jim Thompson's house, at the end of a narrow lane across from the National Stadium, which is the home of the remarkable man who, almost single-handed, made Thai silk world famous. Before his mysterious disappearance while on a walk in Malaysia in 1967, Thompson assembled one of the finest private collections of Southeast Asian art, which is displayed in a number of old Thai-style houses he put together and lived in.

Aside from the perhaps rather specialized requirements of soldiers on leave, Bangkok offers the ordinary tourist a remarkably varied nightlife on a somewhat more refined level. All the larger hotels have nightclubs with dancing and floorshows, and elsewhere in the city there are many pleasant little bars (including a faithful replica of a British pub) and also the usual clamorous discotheques. The area around Patpong Road, near the Dusit Thani Hotel, is a particularly popular section with visitors as well as local people. By day this area presents a sober, business-like appearance, but by night it reveals itself in true colours as the closest thing to an entertainment district that Bangkok has to offer, with everything from jazz bands (mostly Filippino) to Thai girls dressed in bunny costume.

While the average tourist dutifully samples Thai food at least once, he prefers, on the whole, to stick to more familiar fare, and in this respect he is luckier in Bangkok than in many another Asian city. The availability of good Western food is a fairly recent development. Ten years ago, a visitor unwilling to risk the mysteries of Oriental food had little choice of places to dine—apart from the big hotels. Today, an American, a Dane, a Swiss, a Greek, a Frenchman, a Japanese, a Korean, a Mexican or a German can remain comfortably within the confines of his own cuisine during his entire stay in Bangkok. Perhaps not surprisingly, many of them do.

Despite the important role that tourism plays in the general economy of Bangkok, the world of the tourist is, all in all, an exceptionally small one, limited for the most part to a few outstanding sights that have received the blessing of the travel agencies, and to a handful of shops and restaurants. Climate, problems of language, and the physical complexity of the city tend to discourage the sort of impromptu exploration a visitor might enjoy in most Western capitals. Yet for anyone willing to take a little trouble, and perhaps risk a mild bit of adventure, Bangkok has much to offer outside the standard attractions. Almost any of the public markets—Bangrak or Pratunam, for example, or the enormous Weekend Market across from the Grand Palace—provide more idea of the real life of the city than the tourist-conscious Floating Market. And throughout the city, especially in the old section around the palace, there are tranquil, uncelebrated temples full of delightful surprises that find no place in any guide book. Whatever their difficulties with Western languages, the Thai, of all Asian peoples, are by far the friendliest to Westerners, or *farangs* as they are called. One meets students eager to practise their English (or German, or French) in the unlikeliest places. Such impromptu exchanges are often refreshing, coming as they do without premeditation. Any visitor to Bangkok can discover more than most tourists ever discover by simply taking some such student along. Communication may be uncertain, even hilariously difficult, but he will see a little of the Bangkok that ordinary residents know.

A number of visitors manage to see Thai classic dancing somewhere, either at the National Theater, in the pavilion in front of the National Museum, or at one of the hotels and restaurants that present specially edited performances for tourist consumption. Most tourists

The beginning of a traditional Thai boxing match is marked by prayer

Feet, knees, and elbows are all legitimate weapons in Thai boxing

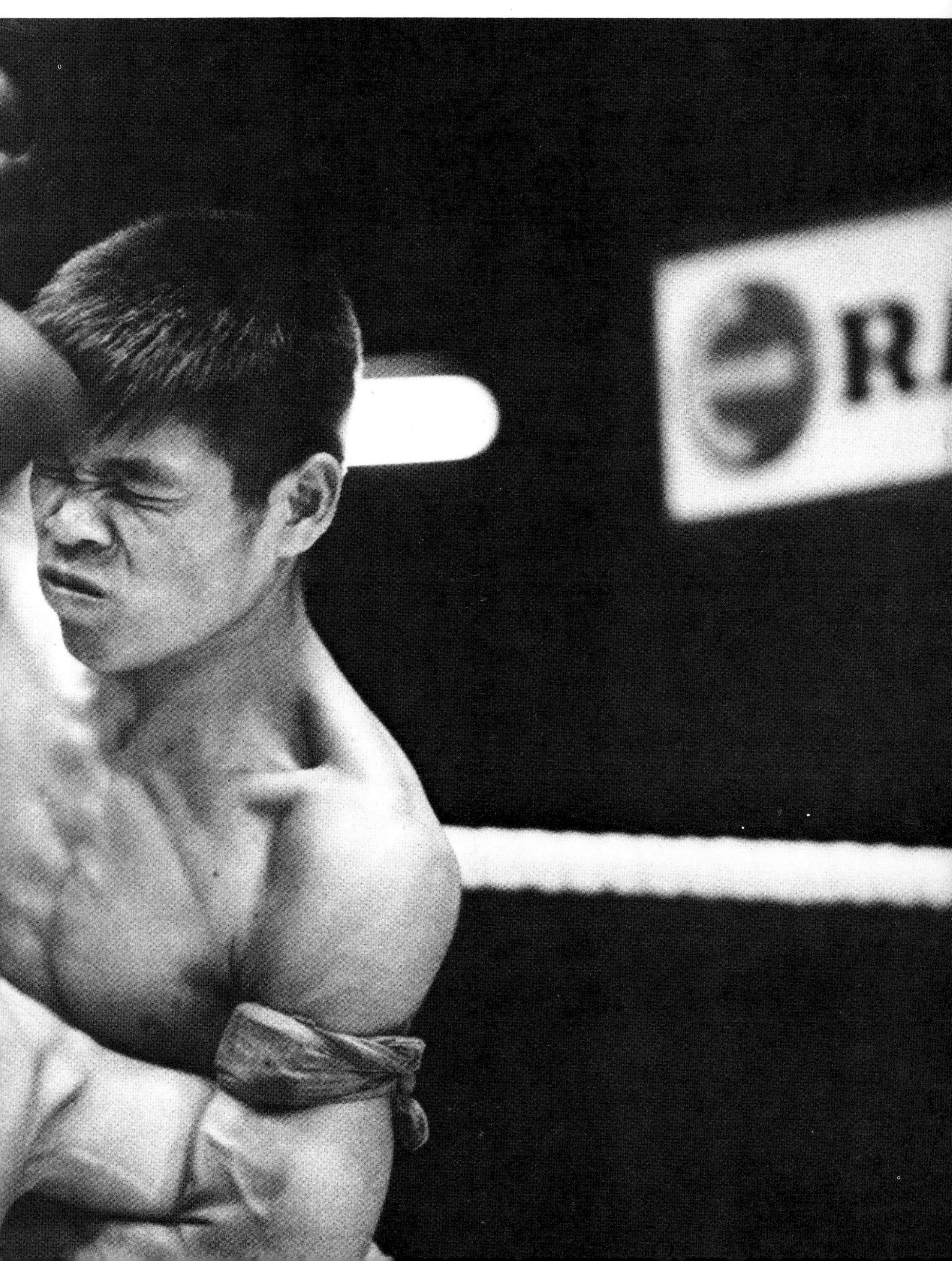

Waiting for customers
outside an antique shop in Nakorn Kasem,
the 'thieves' market' area.
At the Pasteur Institute, attendants
prepare to extract venom for preparation
as an antidote to snakebite

also get a taste of Thai food at one of the several elegant restaurants that have been opened in recent years expressly for this purpose, with Thai decor and staff clad in traditional costumes. It is rare to see a Thai in these places as a customer, unless he is entertaining foreign visitors. The reason is partly the prices, but mostly the food. While often delicious, the Thai food served has been prepared specifically for the Western palate, which means that it lacks about half the usual quantity of red-hot chillies which any Thai considers essential.

Visitors with a little more time often manage to make a trip outside Bangkok, to one of several attractions within easy driving distance. The most important of these is the ruined city of Ayudhya, which even today is still impressive and curiously haunting. On the way to Ayudhya lies King Chulalongkorn's charming Bang Pa-In Palace, carefully maintained still, although it is seldom used by the present king. Another popular side trip is to Nakorn Phratom, where the immense pagoda restored by Rama IV still dominates a landscape of rice fields.

Thanks to improved transportation in the country, quite a few current visitors to Bangkok are venturing even farther afield. Many go north to the city of Chiangmai, noted for its interesting handicrafts and beautiful girls, and also for its cooler climate. There are now several daily flights by Thai Airways to Chiangmai, as well as an overnight express train service. Even larger numbers of visitors are tending to go to Pataya, a resort on the Gulf of Thailand about two hours' drive from Bangkok. Ten years ago, Pataya was a somnolent fishing village that attracted only the occasional weekend visitor. At that time the favored hot-weather retreat for Bangkok people was Hua Hin on the other side of the Gulf where the king has a summer palace and where the court goes to escape the heat of the capital. The Bangkok building boom hit Pataya as well, however, and now the former village has several first-class hotels along the beach and a collection of lively bars and restaurants. The king also spends many weekends at Pataya, drawn there by its excellent sailing and atmosphere of general informality.

When they are not sightseeing, tourists are shopping for some of the numerous handicrafts of the country—silk, of course, in the bold, splashy colors that made it famous; durable handwoven cottons; celadon stoneware, copied from ancient Chinese glazes; carved teak figures from Chiangmai in the north; star sapphires from mines in the south; and sets of locally made bronzeware vessels with Thai designs. And there is a miscellany of other goods such as Thai and Chinese antiques, niello-ware (silver inlaid with a black alloy), paper-thin silver bowls, lacquer, dolls, stone rubbings, and basketry.

During their stay in Bangkok, few tourists meet or talk to any Thai at all except guides, hotel and restaurant staff, and shop assistants. In a somewhat different category, however, are the American soldiers who come to the city from Vietnam or from up-country bases for brief but strenuous holidays. How long these visitors will continue to flow in, is at present a debatable subject. Debatable, too, is the quality of their influence, but they are unmistakably now a part of the city's life and cannot be overlooked. It was largely for their benefit, and not for other tourists, that the New Petchburi Road blossomed into the garish kaleidoscope of amusement that it is today. And even if the soldiers were to leave tomorrow, their effect is more than likely to linger on in some of the whimsical names given to bars and massage parlors, and to the apparently endless number of small hotels built for their use. One suspects that the thousands of girls who deserted provincial villages for the remunerative charms of Jack's American Star Bar, the San Francisco, the Whynot, and Dr. Ward's Massage Parlor will not be inclined to return too quickly to the drudgery of the rice paddies.

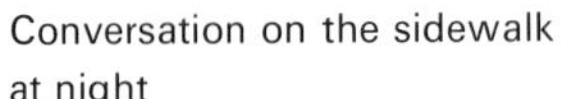

Conversation on the sidewalk at night

The final selection of candidates in the 'Miss Thailand contest — one event in an annual fair

Beauty contests play a
prominent part
in Bangkok life. These girls await
the judging

THE FARANG WORLD

Farang is a Thai word derived, in the opinion of most linguists, from the native pronunciation of 'francais.' It came into currency during the Ayudhya period when a large number of French soldiers were present both in the capital and as a garrison near Bangkok. The term was originally used to denote only Frenchmen. In time, however, it became more all-embracing and is now the word used to designate any non-Asian foreigner.

All Asian countries have some such word, and thanks either to xenophobia or bitter colonial memories the word usually has a decided ring of contempt to it. Thailand is a happy exception. Spared European colonization in the era when its neighbors were being parcelled out among the European powers, it has also been spared the anti-Western prejudices that color life in those other countries even today when colonialism has vanished. The result in Thailand is that a large number of Westerners have found it a congenial place to live in. They began to come to Bangkok, we may recall, in the reign of Rama III (1824–51), and they have been coming ever since. Today the city has a large population of *farang*s in more or less permanent residence.

Both then and in more recent years, the foreigners have made substantial contributions to Bangkok life. *Farang* missionaries introduced into nineteenth-century Bangkok its first printing press, its first newspaper, its first Thai typewriter, and its first girls' school. Modern medicine also owes its origins to them, a fact reflected today in hospitals such as the Bangkok Christian, St. Louis, and the Seventh Day Adventist. In the present century, other Westerners have been equally influential. It was an American, for example, who revived the silk industry. Jim Thompson came to Bangkok in 1945 with the U.S. Army and discovered the shimmering fabric that was then being woven in decreasing quantities by a group of discouraged artisans. Almost single-handedly he developed a world market for the silk and turned it into a major export item that is now probably the country's most famous single product. And it was an Italian named Corado Ferocci who popularized Western art and inspired a substantial number of the present generation of young Thai painters. A sculptor, he arrived in the reign of Rama VI and is responsible for several of the city's major statues, including the one of Rama VI at the entrance to Lumpini Park. Ferocci also acquired a Thai name—Silpa Bhirasri, and had a long career as a teacher in the University of Fine Arts, during which he encouraged many of his students to work in nontraditional styles.

The *farang* world of modern Bangkok is a cosmopolitan and highly varied one, made up of a large assortment of nationalities and activities. Broadly it may be divided into business and official communities, but these in fact can be subdivided into many smaller groups. In the official category, there is the large diplomatic corps, representing forty-one nations; the representatives of the Southeast Asia Treaty Organization (SEATO), of which Bangkok is the headquarters; such international groups as ECAFE, UNICEF, and UNESCO; the American military advisory group (JUSMAAG); and aid organizations from several countries. The multinational Mekong Project, which aims at controlling the Mekong River to make it serve the various nations through whose territories it flows, is based in Bangkok. In addition, a number of Western countries (the United States, England, France, and Germany) have permanent cultural and information agencies in the city, and sponsor frequent visits by writers, actors, and musicians, as well as teachers in Bangkok's five universities.

Westerners may be found living all over the capital, and there is no part of the city that can be described as a distinctly *farang* section. Nonetheless, they have traditionally tended to concentrate in one section or other ever since they first began arriving in large numbers. In the early part of the present century, and until after World War II, the majority of foreign residents lived near the river—especially on the lower part of Sathorn Road where it meets New Road. Today, the largest number can be found in the area known as Bangkapi, on either side of Sukumwit Highway extending from the Erawan Hotel intersection to the Prakanong Bridge. It was in this district that Bangkok was introduced to such twentieth-century innovations as the supermarket and the bowling alley, both of which are now patronized by as many Thai as *farang*. In this district also, were the first apartment buildings and the delights of the private swimming pool. Bangkapi is by no means a Western enclave of the sort that still exists in a number of Asian cities, nor do the *farang*s keep themselves to themselves in the time-honored manner of the Europeans in the East. An unusual number of Europeans, probably more than could be found in any other Southeast Asian city, live almost entirely 'Thai style,' and many of them plan to end their days in Thailand, which has come to seem more like home to them than their native countries. No Thai children attend the International School, an American-style institution that offers twelve years of education mainly in preparation for entering American universities: but this is not an example of segregation. It is merely a reflection of the fact that Americans—who constitute the majority of resident foreigners—do not follow the European custom of sending their children home to boarding schools when the parents live abroad. Socially, integration is probably more complete in Bangkok than anywhere else in Asia. There is no reliable figure as to the number of Thai-*farang* marriages, but it is plainly sizeable and has been for many years. There is even a club in Bangkok composed entirely of Western women married to Thai men. In addition, that American institution, the weekly luncheon and community service club, has become firmly rooted in local life, with organizations like Rotary, Lions, the Business and Professional Women's Organization, and Kiwanis (an American club resembling Rotary), meeting regularly in various hotels around the city.

The Royal Bangkok Sports Club, is a good example of the cosmopolitan nature of Bangkok life. The site was given to the club by King Chulalongkorn, and its membership reflects nearly all the nationalities resident in Thailand. Admission used to be on a quota system, each country being allowed a certain percentage, and with Thai members, of course, in the majority. In its early days the club was strongly English in tone, and one of its contributions to Thai life was the introduction of horse racing, using the small ponies that had already become popular in Malaya. The sport quickly caught on, and on Saturdays, which are race days, the stands of the Sports Club are crowded with members. The general public is also admitted. To meet the enormous popular demand, another racetrack, the Turf Club, was later established across from Wat Benchamabophit with a membership that is largely Thai.

To judge from past accounts, *farang* life in prewar Bangkok contained few reminders of existence back home, and was a world, for all the Western innovations of Rama V and Rama VI, still overwhelmingly Thai. This can hardly be said of the life of the present-day foreign community. Today, Bangkok has become so internationalized—a more accurate word, really, than Westernized—that a foreigner could, if he wished, live a life only marginally different from that in any large American or European city. There are modern, air-conditioned apartments, supermarkets carrying nearly all the familiar Western foods, restaurants that offer practically every variety of cuisine from hamburgers to *coq au vin,* and an almost nightly round of cocktail parties, dinners, and receptions. The average *farang* resident partakes of most of these familiar amenities (as does the average Westernized Thai), in addition to some that may not be so customary in London or Paris or Chicago. By Thai standards, life in Bangkok is not cheap for a Westerner, but by the standard of most European and American cities it is possible to live far better on far less. Locally produced foods are cheap and plentiful, and there is no servant problem.

The typical foreign family in Bangkok today lives either in a new apartment (several hundred apartment buildings have been put up in the past few years, and their tenants are almost entirely *farang*), or in a spacious house. The family has at least two servants, often more.

THE CHINESE WORLD

The Chinese have been described as the Jews of Southeast Asia, the point being that while they can be found in every large city in the area, and have often been there for many generations, they have retained their identity and stubbornly refused to be assimilated by the native majority. Tragically, like the Jews, they have often been the scapegoats in times of trouble, and they have also been discriminated against even at the best of times. All this is true to some extent in Thailand, but far less so than in any other country in the region. Though many of the Chinese of Bangkok do live in a fairly insular little world of their own, in general there has been a remarkable degree of assimilation, and there has never been any of the acute racial bitterness that has flared up in such states as Malaysia and Indonesia. Intermarriage between the Thai and the Chinese has been going on for many centuries, and it has been estimated that a majority of the Thai population of Bangkok is at least partly Chinese. Chinese and Thai cultures have become so intermingled that in many cases it is impossible any longer to separate them. This has been partly the result of deliberate planning, especially in more recent years. Chinese is not taught in the public schools, which means that the younger generation is required to learn Thai, and there has also been an official program to encourage the use of Thai rather than Chinese names. Moreover, Chinese immigration has been drastically cut, so that deliberate isolation will become increasingly difficult as the years pass.

As a result of all these factors, the present Chinese world of Bangkok will possibly vanish altogether in a couple of generations, or will be diluted so as to be almost unrecognizable. At the moment, however, it is still very much a visible aspect of the city, as any visitor to the district around Yawaraj Road will quickly perceive.

This area around Yawaraj Road is the same place to which the Chinese who occupied the Grand Palace site were removed when the city was founded, and it is still the center of a very large part of the city's commerce. Although at first glance, and maybe even at second, it appears hopelessly chaotic—a maze of streets, some of them nothing more than alleyways, and continually filled with noisy crowds—it is actually compartmentalized to a remarkable degree. Whole streets or neighborhoods, for example, are devoted to a single type of product, so that when one knows the district, one knows where to go for bathroom fixtures, for electric generators, for household appliances, for fabrics, for automobile parts. All these items can, of course, be found in other parts of the city (usually at shops whose head offices are to be found in Yawaraj), but the prices are sufficiently lower in the old section to make a trip there worthwhile for the average shopper.

In Yawaraj is to be found the greatest concentration of gold shops. Gold plays an important part in the life of the ordinary Thai, for it has traditionally been looked upon as the safest way to keep one's wealth. Although a stable currency and reliable banks have done much to change this view among the more sophisticated, it still prevails among people at large. The first thing the average Bangkok resident does when he acquires some extra money is to head for Yawaraj and invest it in a gold chain, priced according to weight. If hard times come, it can always be sold for its true value. And, of course, with greater prosperity, he can reinvest in a heavier chain.

The famous Nakorn Kasem area is also in Yawaraj. There is a good deal of misunderstanding about this district among tourists, mostly because guidebooks insist on referring to it as the 'thieves' market,' suggesting that it is, first of all, full of stolen goods being unloaded at bargain prices and, second, that it is Bangkok's equivalent of the Flea Market.

Actually, Nakorn Kasem is a perfectly respectable little rabbit warren of narrow streets, and while a Thai shopper may discover bargains there, the average Westerner finds the goods just as expensive, and sometimes more so, than in the tourist area. The Nakorn Kasem democratically sells everything from toilets to ironwork, but what attracts most visitors is its reputation as a source of rare Thai and Chinese antiques. It is true that there are many antique shops spilling out on to the pavements with their vast assortment of porcelain, carved wood, Buddha fragments, inlaid furniture, and what, in an earlier day, would have been described, with a kind of desperation, simply as curios.' It is also true that certain sharp-eyed customers have ferreted out genuine Sung bowls and sculpture of true rarity from the dusty collections that had their origin in a thousand derelict houses and in the palaces of impoverished noble families. The nonexpert buyer. however, would do well to heed a word of caution. The faking of antiques, in particular Buddha images, has become a fine art in Bangkok since the prices of such things soared, and even authorities on the subject have on occasion been fooled. Nor are the shopkeepers of the Nakorn Kasem quite as untutored as they may seem. Like most Chinese, especially those in the antique business, they have a good eye for their porcelains, and few good pieces go unnoticed or underpriced.

After gold, probably the greatest attraction in Yawaraj for the ordinary Thai shopper is cloth. The narrow lane called Sampeng is crowded with little shops, most of them selling imported materials, and Bangkok women of all classes can be seen there haggling over the prices. In Yawaraj, and elsewhere in the city, too, for that matter, bargaining is expected and apparently a pleasure, on both sides of the counter. And few shoppers would dream of accepting the first price asked without putting up some kind of struggle.

Of all the characteristics of the Chinese district perhaps one is more insistent than most—noise. Bangkok as a whole could hardly be called a tranquil city these days. But the clamor is higher by several decibels on and off the Yawaraj Road. Drivers seem to blow their horns with more abandon there, loudspeakers in front of cinemas are turned up full volume, hawkers bellow from shop fronts, and in restaurants the waiters carry on perfectly ordinary conversations in voices that suggest an imminent riot. When one resident of the area came into money a few years ago and moved to sedate Bangkapi and the status symbol of an all-air-conditioned house in a vast garden, he found the change unnerving. After several months of the unbearable silence, he turned the house over to a relative and moved happily back to a flat overlooking one of the noisiest intersections of Yawaraj. A particular variety of starling also seems partial to the area. Just where these birds spend their days God only knows, but every night they come to Yawaraj where they roost by the thousands on the electric wires along the road, sleeping peacefully above the racket below.

By no means, however, are the Chinese of Bangkok compelled to live in the Yawaraj district. They are to be found in all parts of the city and in all aspects of life—particularly in commercial life. Perhaps a majority of the shops in Bangkok are Chinese-owned, and while this is changing as more and more Thai enter business it will doubtless continue to be true for some time to come. Anyone who visits Bangkok during the celebration of Chinese New Year—the only time when many of the shops in the city ever close—will find ample confirmation of the numbers owned by Chinese.

The Thai food served in many of the restaurants patronized by local people is largely Chinese in inspiration, and at weddings and banquets and other formal occasions the food does not even pretend to be anything but Chinese. In fact, food is one of the major contributions to Bangkok life. There is a variety of restaurants serving not only the well-known Canton, Peking, and Shanghai cuisines, but also the regional food of less familiar parts of China. Some of these are opulent establishments where the prices match the decor, while others are tiny, known only to a discerning few. In the smaller places the food is generally prepared and served by a single family. Word of such restaurants travels fast among the lovers of Chinese food, and fame is apt to follow rapidly.

Chinese workers having
lunch in a
coffin shop in Yawaraj,
center of the Chinese section

A sign painter in Yawaraj

聖英靈通利

和成興大金行
大金行

Yawaraj Road, one of the noisiest and most alive streets of the capital

Burning a paper automobile as part of Chinese funeral rites

THE BUDDHIST WORLD

An aged Buddhist nun with bowls of food given by people seeking merit

In the street, in temples, at prayer, Buddhist monks are everywhere in the city. The Buddhist faith plays a major and vital role in Thai life

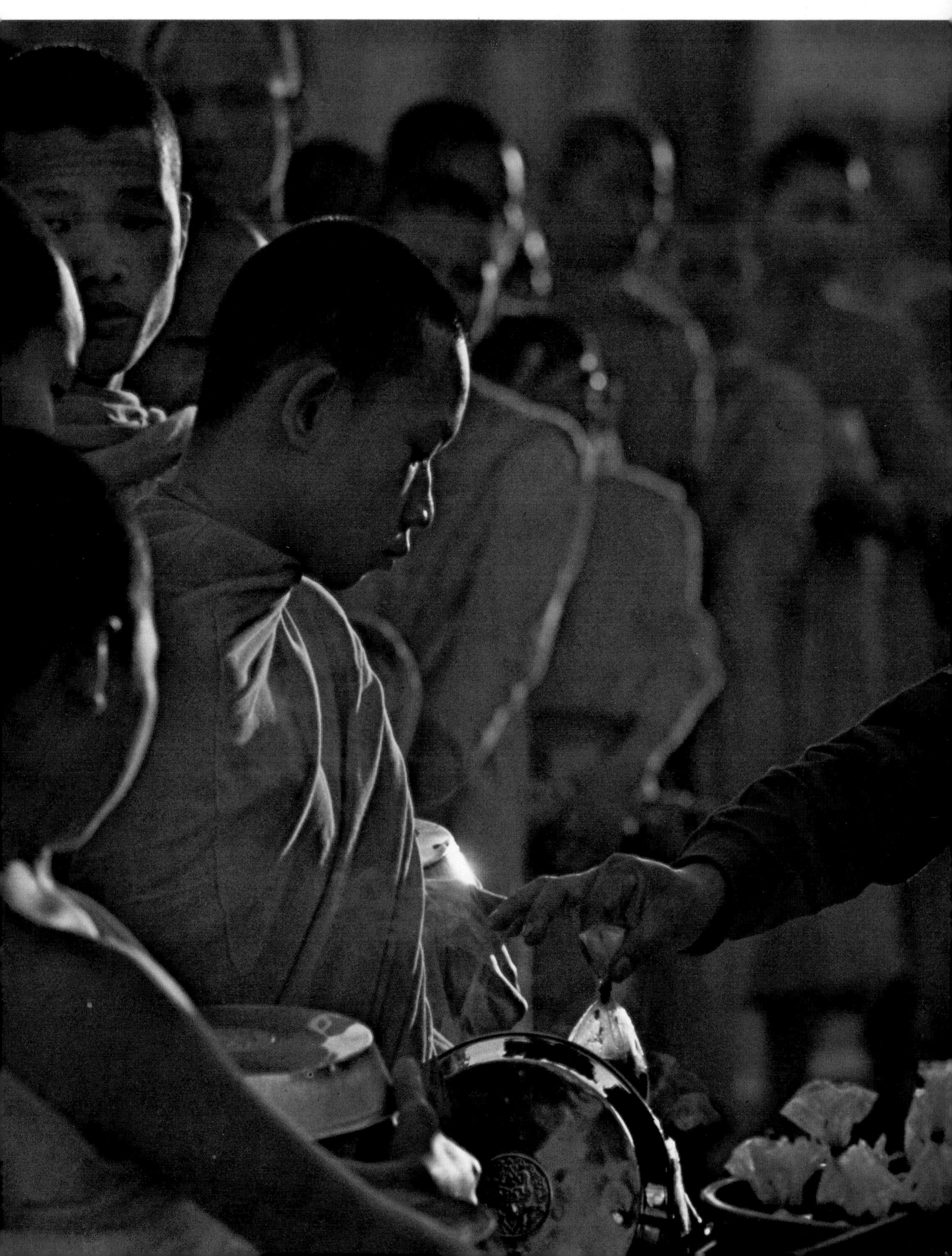

In the courtyard of Wat Phra Keo,
the Temple of the Emerald Buddha, huge
guardian demons
preside over buildings as old as the time of
the first king at Bangkok and as new as the present one

Newly cast Buddhas at Wat Po.
Below, detail of a Chinese stone carving in the same temple

Monks chanting
during a ceremony

Monks in meditation
at Wat Mahatat, the one at the right
a European

A monk taking a bath
in the compound of
Wat Benchamabophit (The Marble Temple)

An old man at
his devotions in
Wat Phra Keo

A Buddhist monk in meditation, seated between images of the Buddha at Wat Mahatat

Monks at prayer
in the Marble Temple

The shrine in Wat Phra Keo
housing statues of former kings is
open only on the present king's birthday in December

An early riser in Bangkok (not so early—say six o'clock) is confronted by a spectacle that, often as one may see it, never fails to impress. From each of the approximately 800 Buddhist temples, or wats, in and about the city stream thousands of priests and acolytes in their orange robes, ranging in age from old men to mere children. All are carrying begging bowls. There is, however, no suggestion of the beggar about them, nor is there the slightest sign of the condescension of charity about the citizens who wait for them all over the city at gates and doorways and on waterside landings with the daily offerings of food. Each is taking part in an ancient ritual, the priest to demonstrate his lack of interest in worldly possessions, the devout donors to earn merit and, hopefully, a better future existence in the long climb toward nirvana.

Buddhism occupies a central role in the life of the ordinary Thai that is difficult for most Westerners to comprehend. Not a dogmatic, clearly defined role, not always even a consistent one (for it is easy to find obvious contradictions between Buddhist teaching and common behavior), but a pervasive one that affects not only religious activities but social and business life as well.

The temples are the visible symbols of this all-embracing influence. Perhaps it is unfortunate that those temples seen by the average visitor are mostly in the category of Royal Temples—meaning that they were built by a king and receive funds for their maintenance. Except for Wat Phra Keo, which has no resident priests, all these Royal Temples perform the functions of ordinary temples but their architectural splendor and historical significance often make it difficult to view them in their true community role as centers of educational, social, and religious activities. A visit to one of the quieter, less celebrated wats will provide a much better idea of the part played by Buddhism, its priests, and its religious groups in ordinary Thai life.

Grand or simple, royal or not, all Buddhist temples are divided into two sections, one where the priests live and perform their private meditative duties, and the other where they perform the public ceremonies. In some temples this division is quite obvious, as at Wat Po where Jetupon Road separates the two. In others the division is not so clearly defined. In any temple, visitors are welcome in the public section, but should not go into the monks' quarters unless they have a friend there, or a specific invitation. Some devout Buddhists visit the public section daily, to hear the priests at their morning prayers, to light joss sticks before the principal Buddha image, or simply to sit and absorb the serene atmosphere which is a characteristic of even the smallest wat. The largest crowds of people tend to be found on Buddhist sabbath days. These days are determined by the lunar calendar and therefore vary each month. At such times special sermons are given by one of the senior priests, often the abbot, on topics of religious interest.

For many years the temples were the only source of education in Thailand. Even today when there are many schools most of the larger ones still maintain their own. In addition, every young Thai man considers it necessary to enter the priesthood for a period of several months, at least once in his life. There is no fixed rule as to the age for performing this duty, but usually it is in the early twenties and almost always before marriage since the retreat is, in part at least, a kind of preparation for assuming the burdens of adulthood. The customary time of year for entering the temple for this temporary noviciate is during the rainy season when, traditionally, there is little to be done in the rice fields. Visitors who come to Bangkok in June or July are almost certain to see the colorful processions that escort the new monk to his temple. There is no longer any established monastic order for women in Thailand, although once upon a time there was, and in up-country villages one still comes across shaven-headed old women in the white robes that the nuns used to wear.

A Buddhist purist—a species, incidentally, far more apt to be found among *farang* converts than among the native people—is likely to be somewhat bewildered as he wanders about a typical Bangkok

Old women praying at the Marble Temple.
Women do most of the decoration
at temples and prepare food
to be given to the monks

The gallery of Buddhas encircling the Marble Temple courtyard. King Chulalongkorn assembled this collection which includes all periods of Thai Buddhist art, and examples from China, Japan, and India

Early each morning in Giant Swing
Square (*top, left and right*) monks
gather to collect food from
people waiting to make this pious gesture.
In the background, Wat Suthat

Devout Buddhist women (*below*) eating rice after a ceremony in the Marble Temple

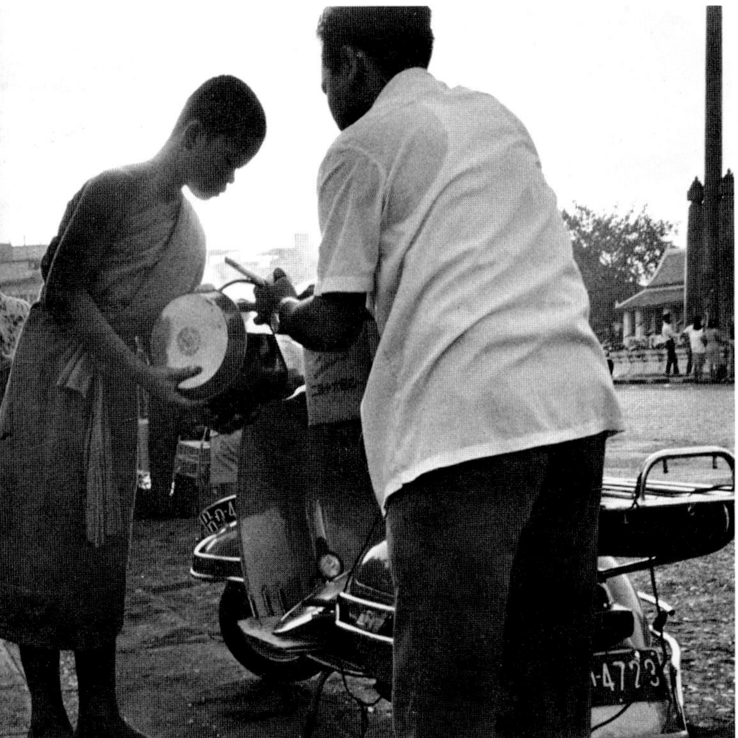

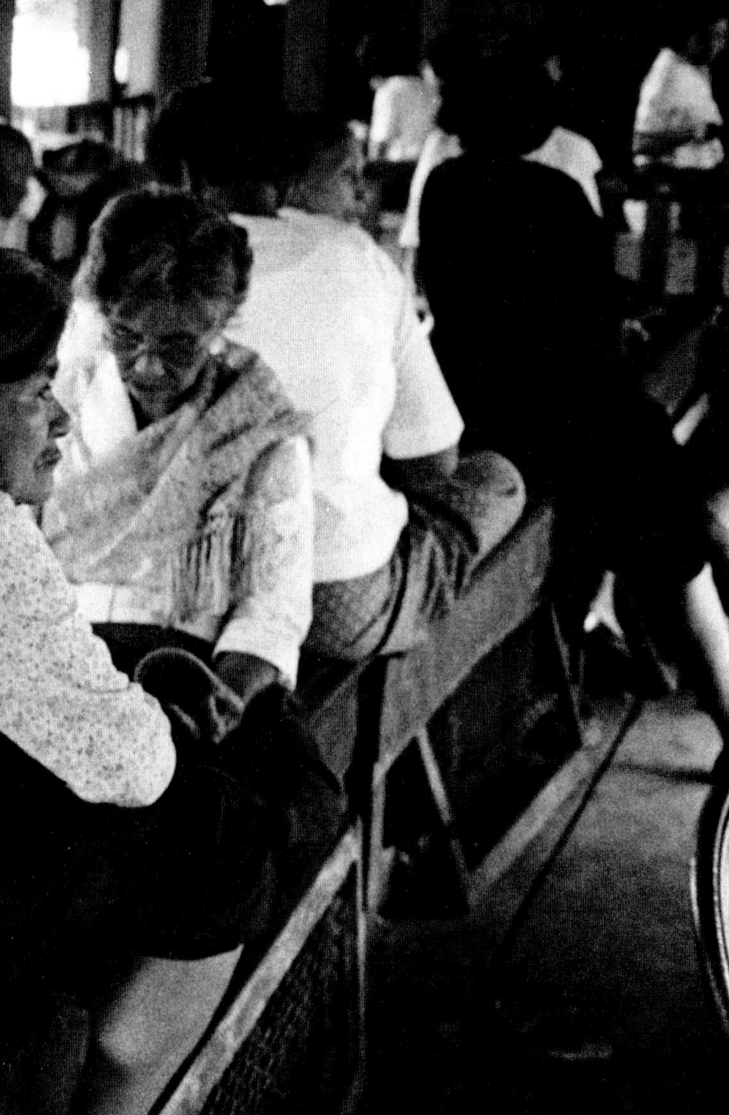

wat. For many of the things he sees have little or no relation to the philosophical tenets of that religion. This is because Thai Buddhism—which is of the Therevada variety, like that of Ceylon—has become intricately interwoven over the centuries with other beliefs, most of them either Brahmanic or animist. Thus, for example, at Wat Po there is a huge lingam (a Hindu phallic stone) on which the faithful regularly stick offerings of gold leaf; and at Wat Benchamabophit (and most other temples as well) there is a prominent spirit house for the guardian spirits, and also a fortune wheel to tell what the future holds in store. Both of these are non-Buddhist, the spirit house being animist. The Swinging Ceremony is purely Brahmanic, as is the Ploughing Ceremony held each June at the Phramane Ground. The most auspicious dates for nearly all important occasions—for weddings or for moving into a new house—are determined on the basis of astrology, at which many Buddhist priests are expert. The average Thai carries or wears some kind of amulet, generally a small votive plaque with an image of the Buddha embossed on it. Depending on its kind and potency, the amulet is believed to protect the owner from a variety of misfortunes ranging from simple bad luck to bullet wounds. A popular source of these amulets in Bangkok is the dealers who assemble every day at Wat Mahatat, behind the University of Fine Arts.

According to Buddhist belief, one's future existences will be either pleasant or painful in direct ratio to the amount of merit earned in the present life, and one of the principal ways of gaining merit is through aiding a temple or its priests. This was the primary motive behind the building of so many temples in Bangkok and elsewhere, and it is also the reason for the ritual of feeding the priests each morning. Perhaps the most spectacular examples of merit making each year are the *kathin*s, which start around the end of the rainy season and continue for about a month, *Kathin*s are ceremonies in which various offerings are made to temples, and during the season there are hundreds of them in and around the city. The Royal *kathin*, when the splendid barges of Rama I sail up the Chao Phya to Wat Arun, is clearly the grandest. But nearly every small temple, however insignificant, is given one of its own, sometimes sponsored by a wealthy family, sometimes by a school, sometimes by a government ministry, sometimes simply by a group of individuals. Several days are given over to the raising of money, which is used to buy a variety of eminently practical items like toothpaste and toilet paper; these are gaily wrapped, and on the day of the *kathin* the group forms a festive procession and carries them to the temple. There is nothing self-conscious about such occasions, and very little solemnity. They are as much a part of ordinary Thai life as eating and sleeping.

Outside of Bangkok, the temples are the social focus of town and village, offering frequent opportunities to meet at ordination ceremonies, cremations, *kathin*s, and fairs, as well as on Sabbath days (determined by the moon's phases) when sermons are given. This is much less true in Bangkok with its innumerable other sources of enterainment. At sermons the audience usually consists of older people, especially women, who are also responsible for most of the food given to monks, and for the decorations before the principal Buddha image. It is tempting to conclude from outward appearances that if participation in wat affairs is any indication of religious strength, then in Bangkok at least, Buddhism is in a period of declinc certainly among the younger generation.

Yet, like so much relating to Buddhism, this would be an inaccurate conclusion. Buddhist beliefs are not so much taught as inherited, and they are probably just as deeply ingrained in Bangkok youth as in the youth of the countryside. A city boy feels just as obligated to spend time in the priesthood, monks are just as much respected, and few Bangkok residents, however worldly, would observe any important event (a wedding, a death, or an auspicious birthday) without calling in a group of priests to chant. And in their daily life they adhere to Buddhist teaching.

THE WORLD OF POWER

The Ministry of Defense illuminated
in honor of His Majesty's birthday

Although he often appears in uniform, the king does not belong to the military world. A constitutional monarch, his function resembles that of other kings elsewhere. Subjects pay their respects in traditional Thai style

H.R.H. Princess Chumbhot of Nakorn Sawan at home in the Suan Pakkard Palace. In the background, the Lacquer Pavilion brought from Ayudhya. Like the king, the princess belongs to the aristocracy and not to the military world. *Below,* Queen Sirikit

If the Buddhist world is difficult for a foreigner to penetrate, and sometimes hard for him to understand, the military world is even more so, since the role it plays is almost totally alien to that taken by the army in most Western countries. Not only does the army defend the country but, since the 1932 revolution, it has played a major part in governing Thailand. In recent years it has been active in the business world as well. From these bare facts, it would be easy to draw misleading conclusions. A number of journalistic visitors to Bangkok have done just that, gaining, and giving, the impression that the Thai government is purely militaristic, or that the population lives in a state of oppression. In fact, the military has become so closely interwoven in the general fabric of Thai life that it is now an integral part of that life, and the familiar Western distinctions between civilian and military hardly exist at all. Many Thai military men live almost entirely civilian lives, employing their rank as part of their title but rarely appearing in uniforms, and behaving in general like ordinary citizens. Nonetheless, the military world constitutes a large part of the world of power.

The Prime Minister of Thailand is a military officer, and so are the heads of most of the numerous government ministries; so, too, are many doctors, teachers, businessmen, and even actors. There is compulsory military conscription – every young man is supposed to spend at least two years in one of the armed services – but this arouses no resentment, for many regard a military career as the best means of personal advancement and would go into service whether they were required to or not. The Army, the Navy, the Air Force, and the Police (powerful enough in Thailand to be ranked almost equally with the traditional services), all have excellent academies for training future officers.

The king, of course, has a place in the world of power, but does not belong to the military world. He occupies a highly significant place in Thai life, and the average Thai regards him as a symbol of the nation. His popularity is attested to almost every day as he and the Queen pass through the city streets on their way to functions and ceremonies.

The traditional center of the military world in Bangkok is the Dusit area, where the Army has its headquarters. Here can be found the offices, and the homes, of many of the leading figures in modern Thailand, and also most of the Bangkok-based soldiers of the Royal Thai Army. Despite the fact that it contains perhaps the greatest concentration of real power in the city, Dusit is a peaceful, old-fashioned district, with none of the nervous energy and feverish building that characterizes the Bangkapi section. Besides the Army, it contains such city landmarks as Vachiravudh College, one of the country's best preparatory schools; Chitlada Palace, the residence of His Majesty the King; and Dusit Zoo, one of the largest and best in Southeast Asia. Its traffic is far lighter than in more modern parts of Bangkok, and its streets are lined with tamarind and mahogany trees; adjacent to the barracks are some of the city's prettiest old Victorian palaces.

Those palaces fortunate enough to have been chosen for utilitarian purposes are generally in a far better state of repair than those left in the hands of their royal owners following the 1932 revolution. Some that are used to house state visitors (Prince Philip stayed in one, and so did Jackie Kennedy) have been meticulously maintained, their preposterous turrets getting regular coats of paint and their formal gardens kept, in many cases, by elderly employees who began their careers in the days when the palaces were really royal. Other once stately homes have not been so lucky, and are quietly rotting away behind clamorous rows of shops, their elaborate fretwork weathered to a silver gray and their stained-glass windows begrimed and cracked. A few years ago, a group of young Thai architects began trying to stir up public concern over the imminent loss of these and other relics of Bangkok's past. The group has had some success in preserving the last remaining segment of the original city wall, but many of the remnants of Victorian splendor are probably doomed by civic expansion.

Senior officers of the Thai
armed forces at a party celebrating
the king's birthday

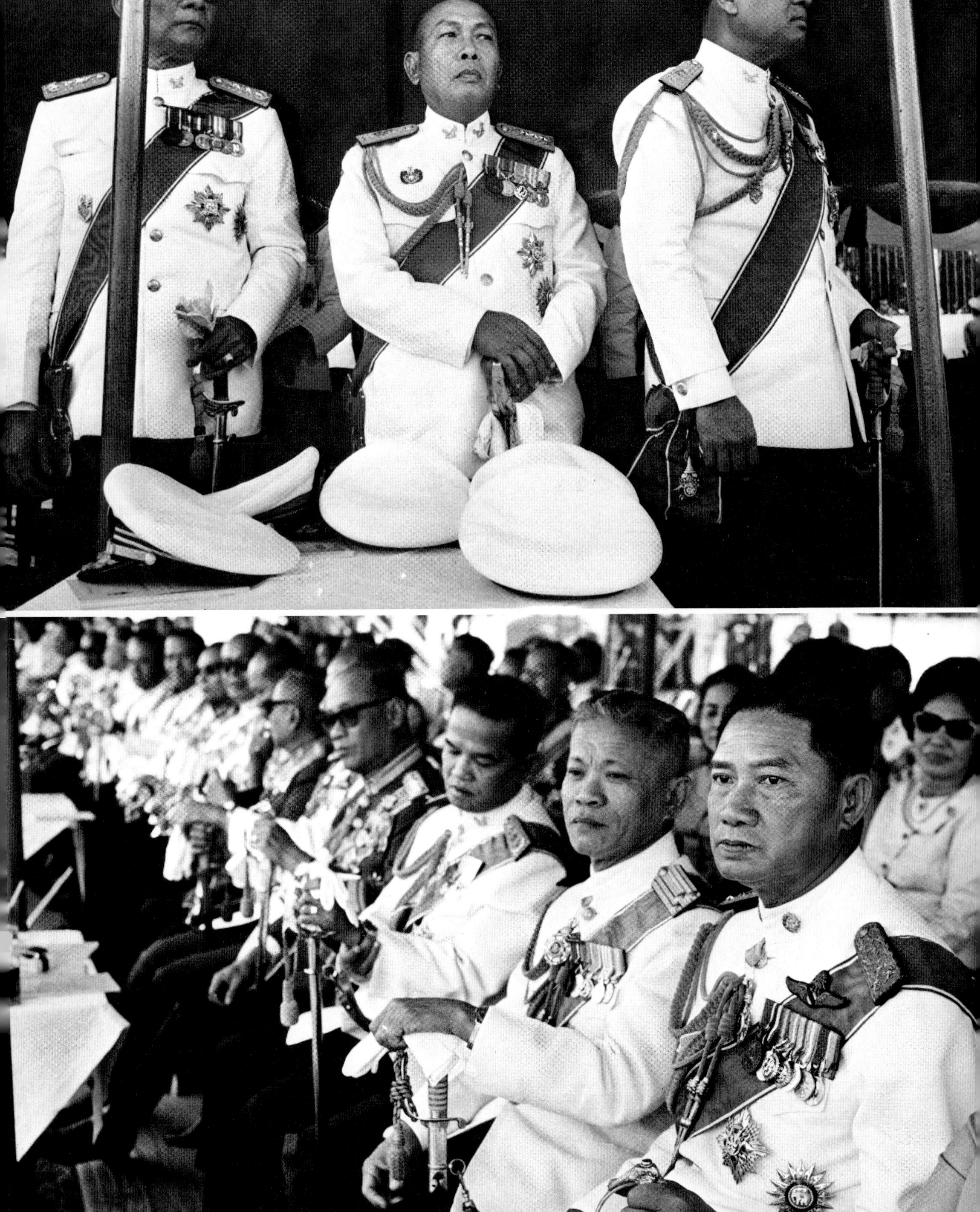

A sentry on guard at the
gate of the Grand Palace

High-ranking government officials
in conversation before
the annual parade on Armed Forces Day

A giant figure of the king
erected in honor of
his birthday

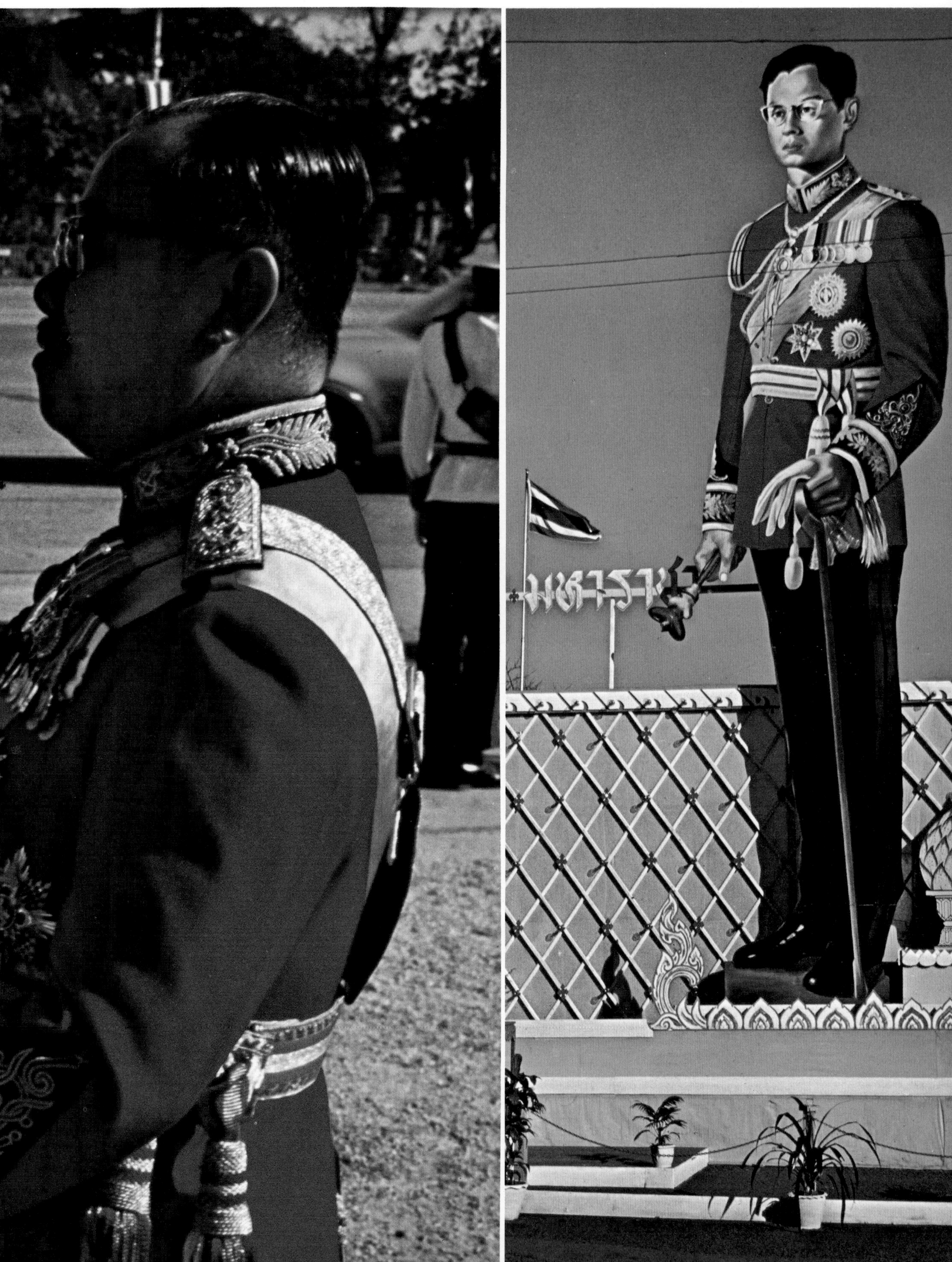

The king's guards on parade.
Below, Her Majesty Queen Sirikit entering Wat Phra Keo on the king's birthday when the royal couple pay homage to the Emerald Buddha. *Right,* an officer in ceremonial regalia celebrates the king's birthday

Spectators watching the king's guard on parade.
The television screen supplements
their view of the proceedings

Officers and soldiers attending a ceremony in honor of King Rama VI whose statue stands near the entry to Lumpini Park

ยันม่าร์

BANGKOK OF THE ORDINARY THAI

Beneath a palmist's advertisement, two men inspecting gems

A Thai wedding. Guests line up to pour lustral water on the hands of the couple seated at the right. Only older and distinguished guests are invited to this ceremony. Friends and young people come to dinner in the evening

The world of the ordinary citizen of Bangkok is not hermetically sealed from the aspects of the city we have examined so far. But it feels like another, quite distinct world of its own. The generality of Bangkok Thai people seldom have more contact with foreigners than one has in passing in the street, and for those who live in areas not contiguous with temple and commerce even that is comparatively rare. With the Buddhist world, all Thai have considerable contact, and with the military in one or another aspect they are also familiar. The Chinese are virtually an integral part of the population, but those 200,000 tourists, birds of passage and sometimes apparently of paradise as well, are far removed from the life of the ordinary man and his family, unless some member of the circle works in an establishment catering to tourists. Yet in a sense, imperceptibly, the worlds blend in varying degrees, the one into the other.

There is no special section of the city in which only Thai people live, but everywhere there are districts in which the majority of people are ordinary Thai. Large parts of their life inevitably remain unseen by even the most determined and perspicacious visitor. And indeed this ordinary undemonstrative life is hard to summarize in brief form. Perhaps one of the best ways to suggest its diversity and complexity is to take a random sample in a selection of vignettes from all over Bangkok. By juxtaposing these, some impression of the variety and atmosphere of Thai living may be forced to emerge.

In a high-ceillinged, paneled classroom in the Faculty of Arts in Chulalongkorn University—the oldest building of the oldest university in the country—a hundred or so students, mostly girls, listen intently while a British lecturer explains the motivations of Hamlet. Shakespeare is no stranger to them. In the previous year they studied *Macbeth*. At the end of the hour the lecturer asks if there are any questions. There will be few, if any: teachers, or *acharns*, are high dignitaries in Thailand, lower only than royalty and priests, and their word is rarely questioned.

Far away in the Bankhen district, near Don Muang Airport, another group of students is working in an experimental vineyard at Kasetsart University. Kasetsart is the agricultural university, and most of its student body comes from the provinces. They study the latest methods in farming, and also experiment with new crops like grapes which, until recently, were unknown to farmers of the central plains. The experimental vineyard has been in operation for some time now, and its discoveries have been at least partly responsible for the fact that grapes are no longer a rarity on the Bangkok market.

Back in the city, at Pratunam Market, a housewife picks carefully through a pile of green mangoes in search of some that are of the proper degree of firmness for one of the numerous Thai dishes that call for unripe mangoes. Like most Thai, she and her family much prefer the green to the ripened fruit. Pratunam means, literally, 'water gate.' Thai place names generally tend to have a singular logic, even if it isn't immediately apparent, and this is no exception—Klong San Saep, one of the city's major canals, is controlled at this point by locks, and the area that grew up around it sensibly took its name from this fact. It is probably the most popular shopping center for ordinary Thai. Apart from the food market, to which fresh supplies come daily by both *klong* and road, it has numerous household supply and clothing shops, as well as a half-dozen of the city's leading cinemas. Late at night, people come to the area from all over the city for a midnight snack, for the noodle shops in the market are highly regarded.

After selecting her green mangoes, the housewife will probably buy a few staple foods—salted fish, some pork, vegetables and, of course, rice. And then before boarding a bus for home she will probably indulge in a little wistful window shopping. She has to be careful with her expenditure for her husband's monthly salary is only 1,000 baht (US $50) although he has a decent job in the civil service. And there are three children to feed, clothe, and educate.

At the Pleonchit Shopping Arcade, near the British Embassy on the Sukumwit Road, two pretty, purposeful girls debate the merits of

Lustral water being poured
over the hands of the wedding couple.
Marriage ceremonies are usually
held in hotels, never in temples

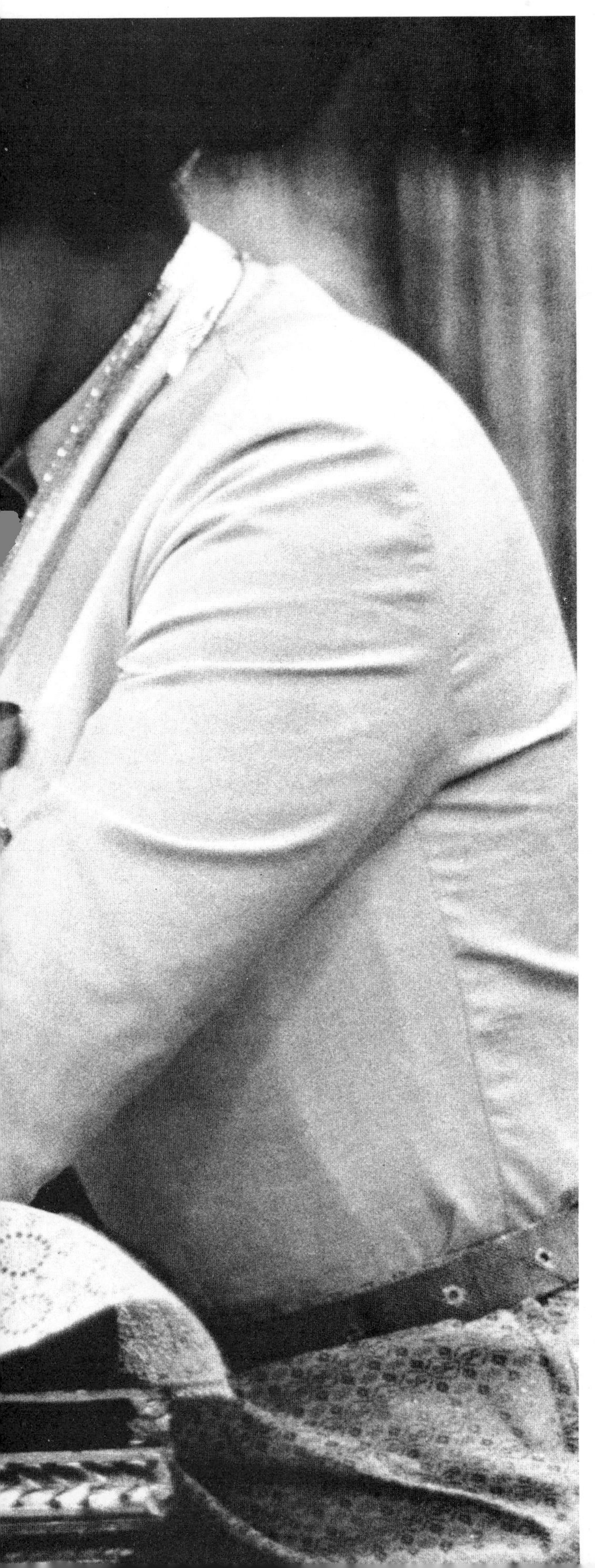

a new hair style pictured in a shop window. Except for the fact that they are Thai, they are identical to the sort of girl one would see on any London or New York shopping street. Their skirts are of the fashionable length and they carry good Italian handbags. Their faces are skillfully made up according to the latest dictates of *Vogue*. Both of them are the daughters of successful businessmen, and both have been educated abroad, one in America, the other in Switzerland. Neither has to work, but they are considering trying to find something 'amusing' to do—public relations at one of the new hotels, or a job with an airlines company—to escape from the rather oppressive atmosphere at home, where their grandmothers look with undisguised distaste on their Western ways, and even their understanding mothers are sometimes bewildered by their interests. Fortunately, things are not quite as difficult as they used to be on this score, for a number of their school friends have also studied abroad, and at least they can commiserate together. Both of them have toyed with the notion of marrying a *farang*, theoretically rather than realistically, but neither is likely to do so. In a couple of years they will make good matches with the sons of other successful businessmen, who will probably be friends of their fathers, and known to them since childhood.

On a muddy lane off Dindaeng Road, a gang of scruffy, semi-clothed little boys try to think of something to do. Surrounding them is a vast inflammable collection of shanties ingeniously put together from packing crates, corrugated iron, bits of lumber scavenged or stolen from building sites. None of the people living here pay rent, have permission to live in the area, or know where they would go if they were forced to leave. Few of them are included in any census of Bangkok. An indescribable smell compounded of stagnant water, fish, human excrement, and poverty, clings to the whole area. The mothers of most of the boys are out working as laborers on some construction project, for which they receive from fifteen to twenty baht a day. Some of the boys have fathers, who work as laborers too, or as drivers of the three-wheeled vehicles known as *samloh*s; some of them have never seen their fathers. Legally, the older boys are supposed to be in one of the state-run schools, but this is difficult to enforce in a neighborhood of this kind, rarely penetrated by outsiders. When outsiders do come, they are likely to be policemen in search of something more serious than a truant. Since they could walk, all the members of the gang have been allowed to roam pretty much where they wanted, the older ones taking care of the younger. There is nothing about the more basic side of life that they do not already know. Most of them will commit a petty crime soon and at least one will commit a serious offense.

In a private clinic off the Sukumwit Road, a young surgeon informs a patient that an operation will not, after all, be necessary; a recently discovered course of treatment will probably clear up the problem. The doctor is a graduate of the Chulalongkorn University Faculty of Medicine. He received a government scholarship to study and do intern work for eight more years at Johns Hopkins in the United States. He is as good in his field of internal medicine as almost anyone of his age in either America or England. In the first of those countries, with his skill and training, he would be earning at least two thousand dollars a month; in Bangkok, his salary at the university, where he teaches, is around one hundred and fifty. Like many of his classmates who studied abroad, he was tempted at one point not to come back, but homesickness, together with a sense of duty, brought him back to Bangkok in the end. He puts in a full day at the university and then, from four-thirty to seven, sees private patients in his clinic. This supplements his income, but not a great deal; his average charge for consultation is only a few dollars.

At the site of a half-completed office building, a construction engineer goes over the plans of the building, which will be eight stories tall. Fifteen or twenty years ago, such a building would have been unthinkable in Bangkok, where the water level is less than a meter below the surface and even low buildings used regularly to sink and

At a funeral, relatives and friends pose for a photograph. A picture of the deceased stands at the left

A Thai Buddhist funeral. Guests enter at the left, make a symbolic contribution to the funeral pyre, and leave by the other door. The cremation takes place in a modern crematorium after most guests have left

crack in the old days. Now, thanks to new techniques learned abroad by engineers like this one, an eight-story building is not at all unusual. Several Bangkok colossi rise higher than twenty stories. Like the doctor, the engineer works for the government, and his basic salary is far below the scale a Westerner could command in his own country. Unlike the doctor, however, he makes a considerable income on nongovernment jobs like this building, and is a direct beneficiary of the construction boom that is transforming Bangkok. He lives with his wife and three children in a ranch-style house in the Bangkapi area, drives a Jaguar, and plays tennis at the Royal Bangkok Sports Club in the evening. In the past, such Western tastes were confined to a very small segment of Thai society—largely to those members of the royal family and wealthy merchant families who went abroad to study, most often to England or France. In the postwar age of the scholarship, however, the group is rapidly enlarging. Nowadays, hundreds of young Thai—not only engineers, doctors, architects, and teachers, but also artists, dress designers, soldiers, businessmen, and hairdressers—are returning from abroad (usually from America) every year, bringing with them ideas that range from the miniskirt to dating girls, or a passion for Danish furniture.

Not all young Thai have been infected by the flood of new tastes, however. In a government office not far from the Phramane Ground, a young typist sits in a large room with about thirty other girls. She is wearing a modest white blouse and a dark skirt that comes well below her knees; not a uniform, strictly speaking, though it almost amounts to one since all the other girls in the office are wearing the same thing. Her hair is simply done and she wears hardly any makeup. She is not particularly shocked by the other girls she sees in films and even on the streets of Bangkok in the middle-class section where she lives—those 'modern's girls with their painted eyelids and their towering hairdo's and their skimpy skirts. For her they simply belong to another world, as remote from hers as is that of a geisha from a Tokyo housewife's. Her salary is small, perhaps $35 a month. She is not a very good typist, not good enough to get one of the higher-paid jobs in a business company. Even if she were offered such a job, however, she would think twice before accepting it, for the civil service offers numerous benefits to the thousands of people it employs in Bangkok. It offers security, for rarely, if ever, is anyone sacked; and it has various arrangements whereby civil servants can purchase land on time payments at very low interest rates; and it provides a pension after the age of sixty. Finally, and perhaps most importantly, government service carries a very high degree of respectability, reflected in the fact that the Thai word for civil servant is usually translated into English as "official,' whatever may be the duties involved. The typist in the government office is unmarried, and her family is old-fashioned in its view of social relations between the sexes. On holidays she sometimes goes to the cinema with other girls from the office—always in the afternoon, of course—but more often stays at home reading romantic stories in women's magazines. Her favorite plot concerns the poor orphan girl with a cruel stepmother who meets, and finally marries, a handsome young man who turns out to be a prince. Perhaps it is fortunate that this is her favorite, for in Thai magazines, with slight variations, this is the basic plot of most of the stories she is likely to read.

On a rather crudely constructed movie set in a residential section of the city, an actress waits impatiently for the director to commence with the shooting. In some ways her rise to fame has been as remarkable as that of the typist's favorite heroine, though in her case the prince was a shrewd director who spotted her four years ago selling fruit in the market in a northern town. Since then she has come a long way, and if she is not quite in the top rank of Thai film stars, she earns at least enough to support her parents, six brothers and sisters, and an assortment of relatives. There are three companies making feature-length films in Bangkok, mostly in 16-millimeter, and they produce anywhere from 40 to 100 movies a year. Most of these films are silent, with the

An old coolie in a rice warehouse in Dhonburi across the river from Bangkok.
Right, sewing up bags of rice, Thailand's major export product

In a Thai silk factory. On the right a length of silk is being printed

dialogue spoken by live performers who read from scripts while the film is being shown. Since the average educated Thai prefers Western (largely American) films to local products, the stories the actress plays in are strictly tailored to provincial tastes: elementary plot lines, plenty of violent action, some slapstick comedy, stylized heroes and heroines. At any given moment, she may be filming as many as five or six pictures simultaneously, working for half a day on this one and then going across town to work on another; often she has only a vague notion of what the particular story is, though she can be reasonably sure it won't differ greatly from the others.

Three soldiers, all privates, alight from a bus near the Erawan Hotel and stroll slowly about the shopping center, looking into windows. Although their salary is less than five dollars a month, they are neatly turned out, with starched, carefully pressed uniforms and highly polished shoes. Personal neatness is almost an obsession with the Thai, as is personal hygiene, and no matter how small their income or how squalid their surroundings they manage both to look and be clean. Before starting their compulsory military service, the three soldiers were all farmers in the provinces. For them Bangkok is still a faintly frightening but nevertheless exciting place to be in, though most of the excitement is perforce vicarious. On their salary they could not even afford the least of the glittering, imported goods displayed so temptingly in the Rajprasong windows.

Nor could they afford the flashily dressed girl with false eyelashes who bounces past them and into a hairdresser's, stares of wistful lust following her through the door. She, too, is a provincial girl, possibly even from the same province—maybe even from the same village—as the soldiers, but her experiences in the capital have been of a very different order from theirs.

Starting her career as a waitress in a coffee shop near one of the large American air bases in the northeast, she moved on to a bar in Korat and, for the past year, has been what is locally called a partner in a bar and dance hall on the New Petchburi Road. Nobody is sure exactly how many partners there are in Bangkok's myriad bars and night clubs (one certainly conservative estimate puts it at 12,000) but whatever the figure, it is large enough to cause a good deal of concern in more conservative circles—especially in the case of those girls who work in places patronized mainly by foreigners. Articles have been written worrying about their effect on Thai culture, and social workers have met to discuss the moral implications of it all.

The girl in the beauty parlor gives little, if any, thought to such weighty matters. Between tips and outside arrangements with her customers, she makes far more than a highly placed civil servant, most of which she spends on cosmetics, beauty parlors, and clothes copied from fashion magazines. Her plans for the future are vague except in one respect: she is sure that she will never return to her native province after the wonders of Bangkok.

In a public school, a teacher in her mid-forties drills a second-grade class in the English alphabet. A graduate of Prasarnmit, the largest teacher-training college in the country, she has been teaching for more than twenty years in the elementary schools of Bangkok; during this time she has seen many changes in the school program—most of them, in her opinion, for the better. One such change is the idea of teaching English to very young children almost at the same time they are learning their own language. She is a spinster and lives with an aging, difficult mother in a crowded neighborhood that borders on a slum, part of which burned down last year in one of the fires that regularly sweep through the poorer sections of the city in the dry season. (Chinese New Year's fires they are called by some of the capital's cynics, since there seem to be an unusual number of them just before that holiday when the Chinese, according to tradition, are supposed to clear up all outstanding debts.)

Despite her age, her middle-class background, and her intensely respectable profession, the teacher is not a strong traditionalist; she is

A worker in the Fiat automobile assembly plant, one of many new industrial complexes springing up on the outskirts of Bangkok

A small store decorated with photographs of former beauty contest winners

Mother and child near Din Daeng Road, one of the poorer districts. *Right, klong* dwellers in Dhonburi

in favor of the new freedoms being claimed by young people, and even shocked her mother once by saying that she saw nothing *basically* wrong with a girl going out alone with a boy in the evening. Still, she herself is careful to do all the things expected of a person in her position. When she meets the head of her school, she gives him a very proper *wai* —the traditional Thai manner of greeting in which the hands are pressed together in a gesture similar to the Western attitude of prayer. (The position of the hands indicates the social status of the giver and receiver of a *wai*; the lower person must always *wai* first and raise his hands higher.) The teacher is also careful to keep her head lower than anyone of obviously superior rank, for it is impolite to look down on such a person. And she is careful, too, to dress in the muted pastel colors that are expected of a middle-aged unmarried woman.

An old woman waits in the brutal sunshine on Rajadamnern Avenue, jostled by a heavy crowd on the sidewalk behind her. A well-dressed girl tries to edge in front of her, but the old woman is stronger than she looks. She has been waiting for the better part of an hour, and she intends to have the view she set her heart on. A car with a flashing red light speeds along the empty avenue, and the crowd murmurs with excitement. The smartly uniformed policemen stationed every few yards stiffen to attention. Then they come: first a roaring squadron of motorcycles, and then the great yellow car, followed by other cars. The old woman has eyes only for the first two cars. In the first a slight man with dark glasses, wearing a white uniform, sits alone; in the second, a breathtakingly beautiful woman flashes a dazzling smile. They are gone in a moment. The crowd gives a collective sigh of satisfaction and begins to disperse. The old woman, however, remains standing on the curb savoring what she has seen.

In a private dining room in one of Bangkok's large new hotels, a group of well-dressed, obviously wealthy ladies discusses plans for a charity ball to be held in Amphorn Gardens, a large pavilion near King Chulalongkorn's Dusit Palace. Organized charity, Western-style, is a comparatively recent innovation, but it has become a major part of the social life of the capital's upper class. As in the West, it is a useful means of social climbing for the *nouveau riche*, and at the same time has brought aid to many unfortunate groups (the blind, for example, and the crippled) not usually included in the traditional merit-making activities of the past and the present. The charity round is also a way of gaining recognition from the King and Queen and, perhaps, one of the much-prized decorations given to conspicuously useful citizens. Most of the ladies in the meeting are married to prominent businessmen or government figures; several, however, are wealthy and prominent in their own right, members of a small but very powerful group of Thai women who have successfully challenged the old all-male business world. All are discreetly but expensively dressed in copies of the latest Western fashions, made by their local dressmakers. Ready-to-wear clothes purchased abroad never seem to fit the Thai figure.

In another private room in the same hotel, a young couple kneel and hold out their hands to be bathed in lustral water from a golden conch shell by their wedding guests. They consider themselves lucky to have been able to reserve the room for the wedding, for this is a lucky month for marriage and several dozen may be held on any one day throughout the city. The next month may be unlucky, and the various halls used for weddings will be empty.

Legally, marriage in Thailand requires no sort of ceremony at all; a couple simply have to register the fact with the authorities. Nonetheless, the young couple, like most others, have gone through a number of rites that are traditional: Buddhist priests have come to chant in the morning, and a variety of Brahmanic rituals such as the pouring of lustral water and the joining of the couple with a symbolic cord have been performed. Only older friends are invited to the water pouring, but in the evening almost everyone they know will be asked to a dinner at which the couple will give each guest a souvenir of the occasion. The groom is dressed in Western clothes which, many years ago, replaced the traditional Thai male attire for even the most old-fashioned ceremonies. The bride, however, wears the long embroidered *pasin*, or sarong, and tight, long-sleeved blouse that court ladies wore hundreds of years ago, an elegant costume that will probably be put away in a chest and taken out again only for a few other very special events. After the dinner the couple will spend their first night in their new house, already built in the compound of the groom's family.

In a large, open pavilion in the courtyard of a wat, or temple, a group of mourners is assembled for the funeral rites of an elderly gentleman, whose photograph, taken when he was much younger, looks rather severely down at them from a black-bordered easel. The men wear white suits with black ties and armbands, and the women are entirely in black, but the atmosphere is hardly that of a Western funeral. The guests chatter amiably and sip orange pop, children dash in and out among the seats, and a traditional Thai orchestra plays enthusiastically on its percussion instruments. Were the deceased a young person—killed in an accident, perhaps, or dead in childbirth—the occasion would be more solemn; but the old man in question had lived a long and successful life, distinguished by many merit-making activities, and there is no reason to be excessively mournful about his passage into what will undoubtedly be a better existence. His remains have been kept in this wat for three weeks. They might have been kept even longer, had his family been wealthier or had he been more eminent, the period punctuated by regular evenings of prayers sponsored by various groups. Ordinary royalty is kept at least a year, and in the case of a king much more, before the cremation is finally held. Such prolonged rites are expensive, however, and this family has settled on a decent interval. When the distinguished guest who is sponsoring the cremation arrives, he will place a symbolic log on the pyre, after which the guests will file up the steps of the crematorium to do the same. After the cremation is completed, the ashes of the old gentleman will be taken to the home of one of his children and kept there in a small shrine, honored with flowers and incense on occasions such as the anniversary of his death.

In an adjoining pavilion in the same temple, a Chinese cremation is in progress simultaneously. This is a noisier affair, with much banging of gongs. The participants are dressed in shapeless suits of sackcloth and wear a kind of cap of the same material; banners with Chinese characters flutter in the breeze. Like many Chinese-Thai, the family of the dead person is observing a convenient mixture of their own and Buddhist funeral rites, with the emphasis on the former. The ashes of the deceased will eventually be interred on a traditional Chinese hillside tomb, north of Bangkok where there is rising ground.

A gang of slickly dressed young men—loud shirts, bell-bottom trousers, boots with pointed toes and zipped sides—lounge restlessly in a coffee shop, commenting on the girls that walk past. They are some of the problem children of Bangkok, though most of them are hardly children. They have enough money to indulge their taste for smart clothes, but not enough to have other things they want. They have had enough education not to want a 'low' job, but not enough to get the white-collar job they think they should have. And they have sophistication enough to see that some of the old ways are not relevant to modern life, certainly not to *their* life. But like similar youngsters the world round, they are unable to work out satisfactory substitutes for traditional ways of life. Boys like these are not criminals, but they account for a fair proportion of the petty crime in Bangkok—purse-snatching, burglary, vicious intergang fights that sometimes involve innocent bystanders. Their favorite haunts are the cinemas, the coffee shops, and the bowling alleys. Their families are mostly middle class, sometimes even higher in the social scale, and they share an almost total incomprehension of what makes their offspring so dissatisfied and violent. The newspapers write disapproving editorials about the boys, criticizing their clothes and their hair styles; the government issues warnings to them to mend their ways; older Thai shake their heads in

Children enjoying the varied
amusements of the Weekend Market
on the Phramane Ground

dismay at the latest reported outrage. American movies, television, the foreign soldiers, and the educational system are blamed. Nobody, however, can think of a workable solution. Meanwhile, the boys lounge in the coffee shops, the cinema lobbies, the bowling alleys, suspended between two cultures.

A high-ranking princess, known for her cultural interests, steps forward, cool and poised, while flashbulbs pop, and cuts the ribbon to open a new exhibition at an art gallery. Modern art—that is, Western abstract art—came to Thailand a good many years ago, but met with little local response until the early sixties. At that time a whole group of young painters burst upon the scene, quickly followed by a dozen or so galleries in Bangkok. (The only gallery outside the capital is in Chiangmai, in the north.) The artist of this particular exhibit is in his late twenties, flamboyantly dressed in costume-party hippie style with gold chains and a velvet shirt. Many Thai painters seem to be self-consciously imitating their bohemian counterparts in the West of fifty years ago, perhaps because, like them, they are struggling against a strong tradition. The artist of this particular show is relatively successful, unlike the majority. He studied in Rome—a popular place for Thai art students since it was the Italian Ferocci who provided the greatest stimulus for modern art in Bangkok and who is honored with a statue at the University of Fine Arts, where he taught for many years until his death. The paintings sell well, more to foreigners than to Thai, and fetch good prices.

While irritated drivers behind shatter the hot air with their horns, a taxi driver and a potential customer go through a leisurely ritual of settling on a price in the middle of a narrow, congested business street. A few years ago, the government passed a law that required all cabs to install meters, and a half-hearted attempt was even made to have them used. But it was a losing battle. Certain seemingly entrenched Thai customs have been changed by official dictate—no one now spits out the red betel-nut juice as used to happen all over Bangkok, before the government came out against the practice twenty-five years ago—but the habit of bargaining over taxi fares seems impossible to eradicate. The simple fact is that both parties, passenger and driver, enjoy the palaver, despite all the confusion it causes in the streets.

A three-wheeled taxi, known in Thai as a *samloh*, clatters into a narrow lane off New Road. It is perilously overloaded with boxes and baskets, beneath which sits an elderly Chinese lady in black pajamas. The *samloh* drivers are members of a dying breed, and they know it. First the rickshaw, then the pedicab gave way to the exigencies of metropolitan traffic problems. The *samloh* has been scheduled for retirement for a long time, but it has proved remarkably good at getting last-minute reprieves, partly because of the problem of what to do with all the drivers whose livelihood would vanish, but mostly because the *samloh* answers an urgent need among a large segment of Bangkok's population. Buses don't run in many parts of the city, and taxies are too expensive for the average citizen. But sooner or later, everybody agrees, something will have to be done. And there the matter rests.

A businessman settles himself into a chair in a barbershop for his fortnightly haircut. It will not, however, be the quick, mechanical operation which for most Westerners is simply an ordeal that has to be undergone every so often. For a Thai male, a visit to a barbershop serves much the same purpose as a visit to a beauty parlor for a woman, except that for the man the procedure is likely to be far more elaborate and a good deal cheaper. Besides a haircut, a shampoo, and a shave, the businessman has a massage (either in his chair by the barber, or in a private room by a pretty girl), and has his hair dyed and curled if he feels like it, his ears cleaned, his nails manicured, and his ego soothed—the whole of which may occupy several hours and cost about as much as a single, perfunctory haircut in a New York or London establishment.

Under the vast roof of Lumpini Stadium on Rama IV Road, a crowd drawn from all classes of Thai society settles down to watch a

Left, dyeing Thai silk. Nearly all the dyes now used in the ancient craft are imported from the West. *Below,* a Sunday game of chess near Wat Mahatat

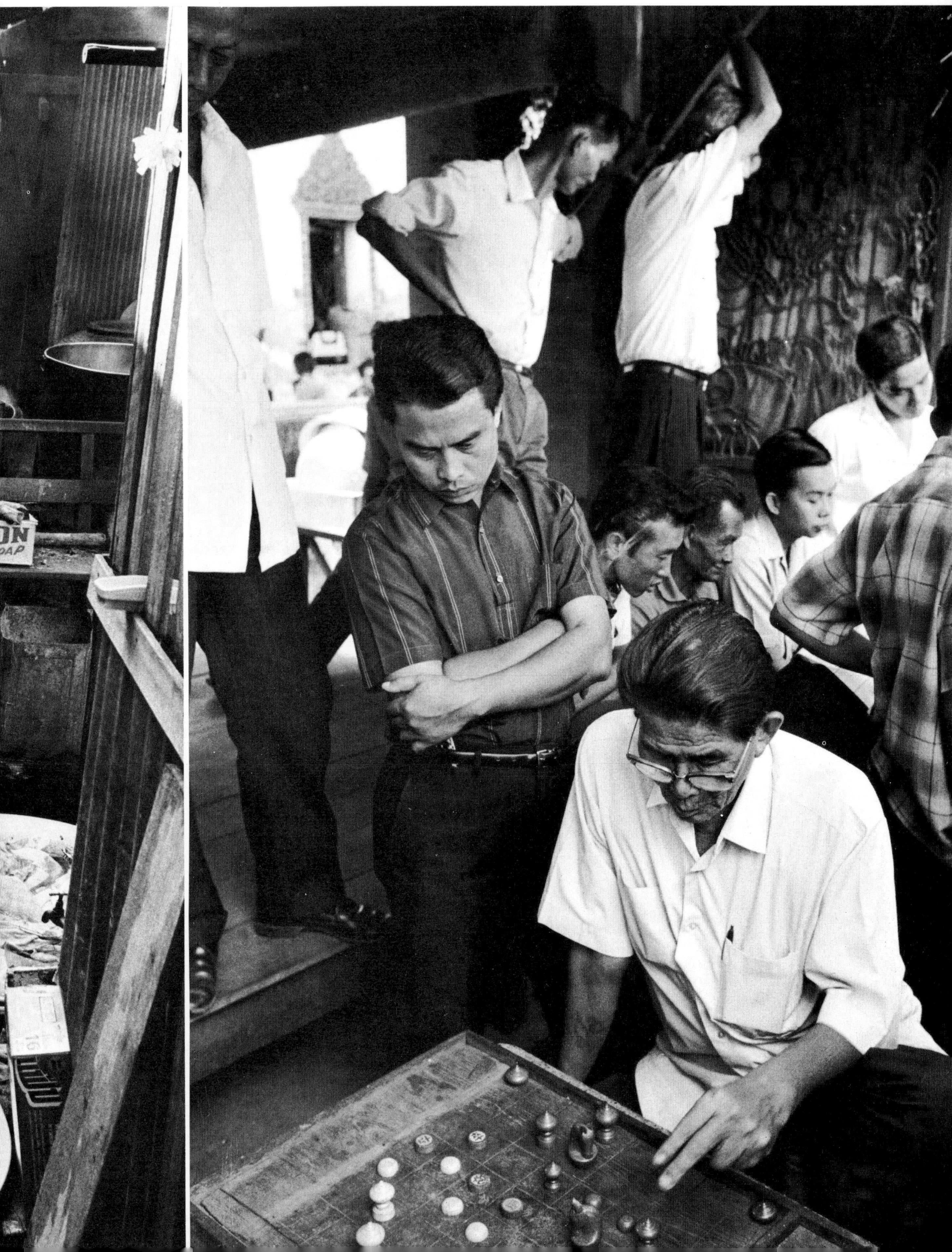

The many spices used in Thai cooking can be bought in small markets from individual vendors. *Right,* a woman sits amid stacks of birdcages at the Weekend Market while her baby sleeps in an improvised hammock

Thai boxing match, perhaps the most popular of all the country's sports. Except for the use of gloves, the observance of timed rounds, and the objective of knocking one's opponent out, Thai boxing has little in common with its Western equivalent. To begin with, there is a strongly ritualistic atmosphere about it. Before fighting, the boxers perform a curious, stylized dance in which they suggest the fight to come and also invoke the goodwill of the spirit world. The entire match is accompanied by music which increases in tempo at crucial moments. Moreover, during the actual fighting, practically nothing is forbidden. Elbows, knees, feet, and any other part of the body may be used to fell an opponent and the ultimate blow is achieved with one of these, far more often than with the gloved fist. The result, however, is less the mayhem one might expect than an oddly elegant suggestion of ballet that is both hypnotic and exciting. Having mastered the art of Thai boxing, it is apparently simple enough for a Thai fighter to become equally skillful at the more conventional form; in any event, two of the recent world flyweight champions have been Thai, and boxing camps throughout the country are full of youngsters hoping to become the third.

In Dusit Zoo, a decorous young couple lounges in a rowboat on a picturesque little lake, and indulge in the closest thing to courting that is permissible in polite Thai society. Of course it includes no sort of physical contact, at least not in a public place like the zoo. Even holding hands is looked upon by the majority of Thai people as a rather shocking Western custom when indulged in by a boy and girl, though between members of the same sex it is perfectly acceptable. The zoo, with its pleasant acres of well-landscaped gardens and ponds, and its large collection of animals, is a favorite spot for weekend courtship, as well as for family outings. Of its animal residents, by far the most celebrated are the royal white elephants, which are housed in a special Thai-style pavilion and treated with exceptional courtesy by their keepers. White elephants are albinos and not, of course, actually white at all but pinkish; to qualify, a specimen must pass all sorts of color tests applied by experts. When an elephant is found that does pass the tests, it automatically becomes the property of the king. White elephants are believed to be a sign of luck, and in the past the kings throughout much of Southeast Asia measured their fortunes by how many they possessed. Not a few wars in the area have been fought over the animals. White elephants were also once thought to symbolize all the best human qualities, so that when some nineteenth-century Thai emissaries to England wished to sum up their favorable impression of Queen Victoria, the highest compliment they could pay that monarch was to note that "her eyes, complexion, and above all her bearing, are those of a beautiful and majestic white elephant."

In Lumpini Park, Bangkok's only other large public garden, not far from the Erawan Hotel, a group of young men assemble on Sunday afternoons for a game of *takraw*, one of the most popular amateur sports in the kingdom. At its most elementary, it simply involves knocking a rattan ball back and forth among the players in a circle, using any part of the body except the hands. This bald description gives little idea of the extraordinary grace and elegance of the game, for even the least skilled players seem capable of marvellously balletic movements that are fascinating to watch. The Sunday players at Lumpini are frequently skilled indeed, and play far more complex games than those that can be seen at practically any schoolyard in the break between classes. In one variation, for example, the object is not merely to keep the ball in the air as long as possible but to put it through a basketball net suspended in the center of the circle. Some of the Lumpini boys may even have taken part in the *takraw* contests at the Asian Games, which formally raised the game to the level of a professional sport.

In the cavernous, echoing terminal building at Hua Lumpong Railway Station, a local train from the Northeast pulls in and the passengers disembark, carrying with them a vast assortment of belongings in small packets and bundles. Among the arrivals is a boy of about

A poster advertising an Italian film forms the background to a *samloh,* the three-wheeled vehicle that replaced the pedicab

seventeen, his wordly belongings contained in an imitation airline bag. He is alone, this is his first experience of Bangkok, and no one has come to meet him for the perfectly good reason that no one knew he was coming. In his pocket, carefully folded and frequently taken out for study during the long journey, is a piece of paper bearing the address of a distant relative of his mother's. The boy would probably refer to him as uncle, though actually the connection is much more tenuous, and possibly not even a matter of blood. Nonetheless, the relative will welcome him, share what food there is, and provide a corner of a room as a temporary sleeping arrangement—all more or less obligatory, no matter how distant the relationship. Perhaps the uncle may even be helpful in finding a job (for that is why the boy has come to the city), with the understanding, of course, that half of what he may earn will be sent back home where there is a chronic shortage of money. Back home there are four sisters and three brothers, along with parents and grandparents and a real aunt or two. Of them all, the boy has been chosen to go to Bangkok because he is considered clever, which means he can read and write, and because he managed to get through five years in the state school near their village. In the village there is no future for a clever boy, and not much of a future for any other kind of boy. But in the great capital there are thought to be endless possibilities. Clutching his bag tightly under his arm, for he has heard of all the evil people in the city, the boy walks nervously out of the terminal into Bangkok's blinding sunlight and incredible noise.

In all Bangkok, there is perhaps only one place, or rather one event, at which one could find a representative sampling of all these different types together. This is the phenomenon known as the Weekend Market, held in the oval Phramane Ground across from the crenellated walls of the Temple of the Emerald Buddha and near the Lak Muang Pillar which King Rama I established as the spiritual heart of his capital. The market begins to take shape very late every Friday night, except when the field is preempted for special celebrations, such as that at New Year. Many of the stallkeepers come by boat, along the river and Klong Lawd, just as they have been doing for a hundred years. Others come by truck, sometimes from hundreds of kilometers away. And still others who live in the vicinity simply walk over, carrying their goods in huge woven straw baskets. Some bring with them poles, canvas, display tables, and cages; most rent what they need from enterprising agents who have semipermanent concessions not far away. By the first light of dawn on Saturday, the usually deserted and dusty field has been transformed into a tremendous show that is part traditional public market, part carnival, part restaurant, part meeting place, and perhaps the most concentrated single display of genuine Thai life a visitor is likely to find in the entire kingdom.

The market only lasts two days. By Monday morning, the field has been returned to footballers, bicyclists, students from nearby Thammasat University, and the ghosts of the seven Chakri kings who were cremated there. But during its brief flourish, the market offers the most varied shopping to be found in the country—everything from a kilo of rice to a flowering *phaleonopsis*, or a baby python—and also the greatest free show, where one can enjoy all sorts of wonders without spending a single *satang*.

On a typical weekend, in the central part of the field, not far from a display of kites dancing in the wind from the top of poles, the sound of drums and flute attracts a crowd of apprehensive-looking people. It is a patent medicine vendor, advertising by means of a free, no-obligation-to-buy fight between a cobra and a mongoose. The medicine the man is offering has the miraculous properties of curing snakebite, alcoholism, impotence—or simple melancholy. Few of the audience will buy it. But they are very willing to while away an interesting half-hour or so. The snakes, huddled together in a basket, are a generally lethargic-looking lot, but every now and again one of them rises, flares its hood, and makes a half-hearted strike at the unbooted leg of the barker. When this happens the crowd backs away and murmurs in delighted

In a new department store. Most of the goods are expensive, imported products. Cosmetics are especially popular

The salesgirl in the department store (*top*) would be likely to buy from her counterpart at the Weekend Market (*lower left*), or from the street vendor (*lower right*)

horror. They all know, of course, that the snakes have had their poison sacs removed, but just possibly, one might have contrived to grow a new set, and then . . .

In the same area, along a cemented walk that cuts across the field, a row of raffish-looking men with sly eyes and foreign faces—Burmese perhaps, or Indian, or maybe even Nepalese—sits before a glittering collection of gems, like some rifled treasury spread out in the sunlight. An old lady with a distinguished, possibly aristocratic face squats in front of one pile, looking long and shrewdly at an enormous red stone that may—or then again may not—be a ruby. Nearby are palmists armed with complex charts and enormous magnifying glasses. Their prices depend on what they see; good news is more expensive than bad.

A cacophony of squawks, squeals, shrieks, and growls leads one naturally to the animal section, also in the central part of the market where there are a good many other diversions. One dealer, who specializes in rare items, has on display (and, of course, on sale) a *bentarong*, a mouse deer, and a couple of jungle cats. For those who may not know, a *bentarong* looks like an unfortunate cross between a bear and something not readily identifiable, a mouse deer looks like a cross between a mouse and a deer (the body of the former and the legs of the latter) and a jungle cat is a loveable-looking spotted creature that would rather scratch your eyes out than be cuddled.

A group of connoisseurs at another stall debates the merits of a collection of Siamese fighting fish. The males of the species (which is found wild in the rice paddies) are highly and incredibly colored, but beauty has nothing to do with which will command the highest price at the market. The popularity of fighting fish with the Thai is due to the astonishing pugnacity of this species of fish, so great that if two males are put in a single container they will immediately do battle until one is dead. The Thai are by nature enthusiastic gamblers, and the idea of fish fighting long ago proved irresistible. Up-country, they also wager over the outcome of beetle fights, using a horned variety that lock horns and push and pull for hours until one is turned over on its back.

In a number of cages in the animal section can be seen blue-eyed Siamese cats, the animals undoubtedly most closely associated with Thailand by foreigners. Unfortunately, Siamese cats are as exotic in Thailand as in England, and have about as much to do with the country as Siamese twins. The average Thai cat fancier would far rather have one of the several domestic cats whose coloration marks them as lucky; a three-colored cat, for example, though the name is somewhat misleading as black and white qualify as colors. A three-colored *male* cat is especially prized since it is not only lucky but also rare since, according to legend, mother cats habitually kill three-colored male offspring. Farfetched perhaps, but no more so than that old chestnut about Siamese cats being guardians of the temples.

Across from the market area along Klong Lawd, in the flower section, a white-haired gentleman who looks like a scholar and is, in fact, a professor at a local university, holds a learned discourse on hybridization with a group of orchid specialists. His stall at the weekend market is kept not so much for profit as to provide him with a place to display his prize blossoms and to exchange horticultural gossip with others who might not find their way to his home. Orchid growing is one of the most popular Thai hobbies, especially among elderly men, and many new hybrids have been produced, including one stunning new *cateleya* named after Her Majesty Queen Sirikit.

Booklovers and students on the hunt for a cheap, secondhand copy of a textbook, gather nearby at the book market, where stalls are piled high with volumes of all sorts. Overlooking the browsers is a statue of the Mother of Waters, from whose long rope of hair a steady fountain pours into a pool.

The food section, occupying about a third of the perimeter of the field, displays an abundance of local produce that is certain to dispel, at least for the moment, any haunting images of a starving Asia. Moun-

Left, a sales assistant waiting for customers in a store. A dancer (*top*) at the Baan Thai restaurant prepares for a performance of Thai dance. *Below*, girls on a *klong* selling food, including meat on skewers

Fortune tellers in the Yawaraj district specialize in reading palms

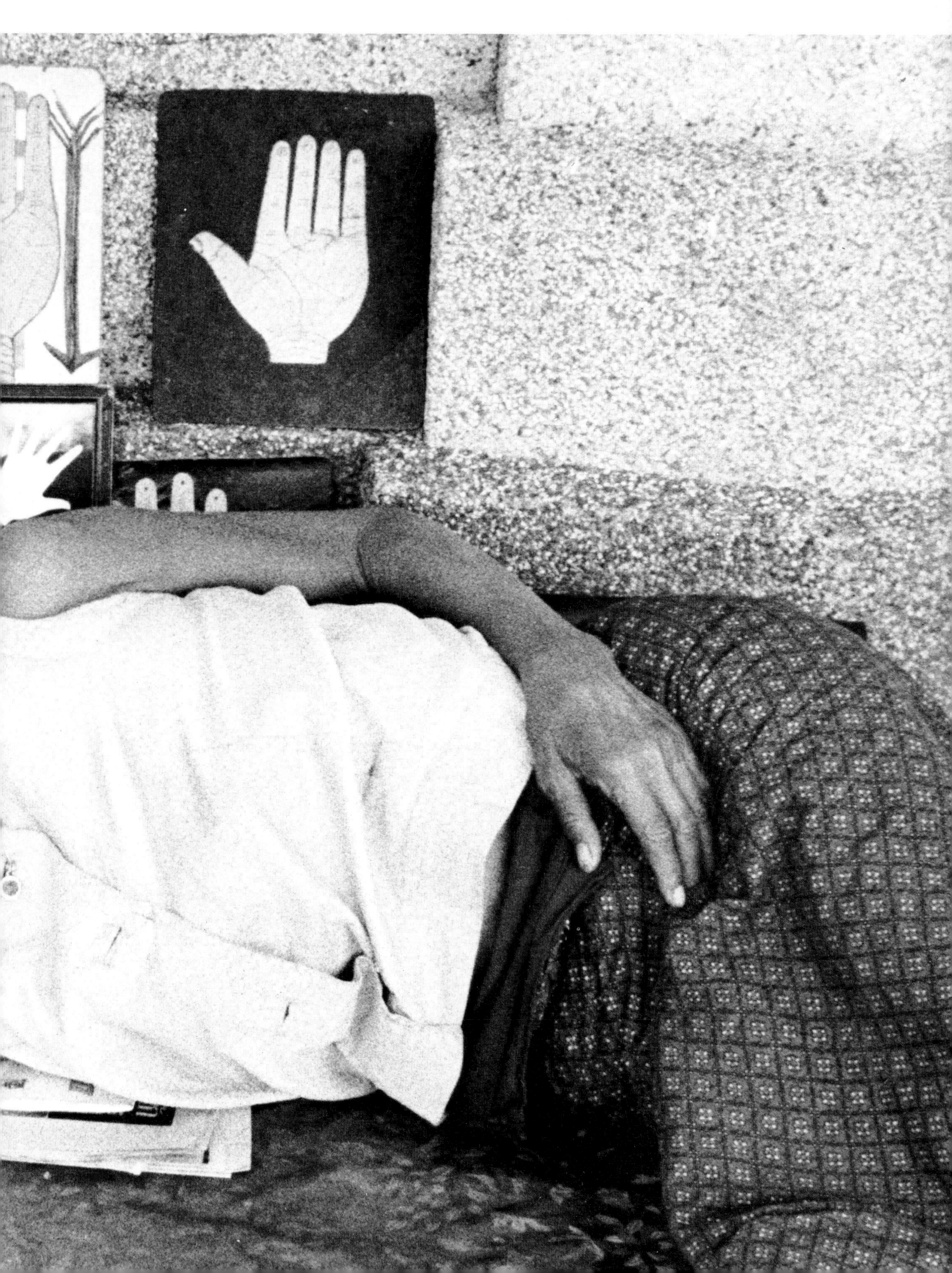

Students at Chulalongkorn University playing a game called *takraw.* The ball is rattan. Behind them is the Faculty of Arts, the original building of the university. *Right,* a girl reading on the sidewalk

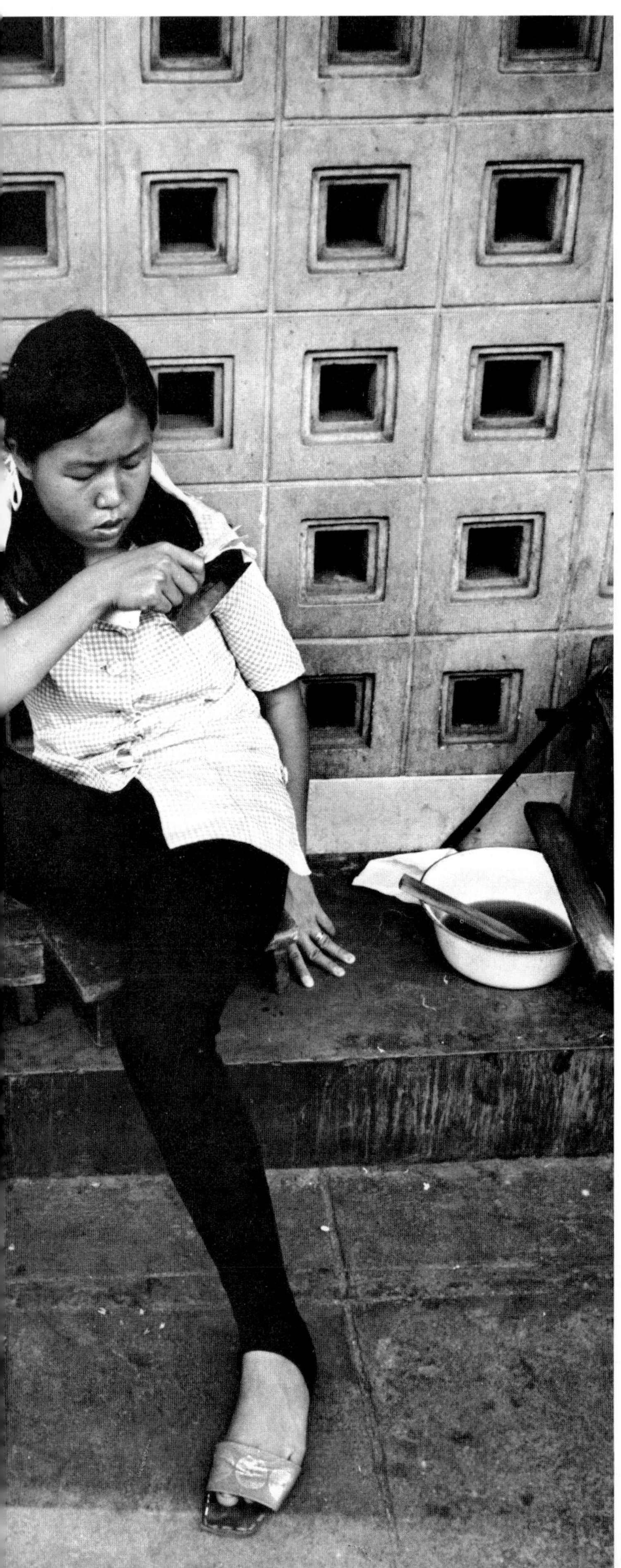

tains of fruit, the year-round varieties—pineapple, mangosteen, banana, grapes, guavas—and, in season, the more highly prized specimens like the mango, and the pungent durian that is repellent to some and ambrosia to others. There are a dozen varieties of fish, dried and salted, and endless numbers of the herbs and spices essential to the complex Thai cuisine. Every few meters a vendor squatting beside a charcoal brazier is producing some delicacy—fried banana or tiny pancakes stuffed with bean sprouts. On a stone found in ancient Sukhothai, the first capital of Thailand, the great King Ramkamheng enjoined his people in writing to be grateful. The inscription is the earliest known example of Thai script. "This *muang* (country) Sukhothai," he wrote, "is good. In the water there are fish; in the fields there is rice." Amid the bounty of the market, nearly all of which comes from the earth and waters of the country, one is inclined to think that the royal observations still hold true, nine hundred years later.

The crowds who flock to the Weekend Market come from all the worlds of Bangkok. There, overlooked by the glittering spires of Wat Phra Keo, they are back, for a brief moment at least, where it all began when Rama I crossed the Chao Phya to found a new era of Thai life. In the great city around them little has remained constant, and almost nothing is predictable except that in the future there will be more changes. Yet, at the market itself it is possible to sense a continuity, a relationship between past and present that can be found in no other single place in the city. In the rest of Bangkok one feels squarely in either one or the other, in the past or in the present, and a kind of void seems to lie in between, making transition difficult. It is this, among other things, that makes it hard to define the city's character, to pin down its elusive personality; for one is uncertain whether the emphasis should be on the more obvious modern aspects or on the more celebrated picturesque features. Is Bangkok the rising new skyline of Bangkapi, or the timeless towers of the old Grand Palace? Or is it both? And, if so, what is the bridge that joins them?

For at least a partial answer, go to the market on a Saturday, preferably in the late afternoon when the human traffic is heaviest and the ornamented roofs of Wat Phra Keo are ablaze in the late light, like some fantasy structure from an ancient legend. There is nothing fantastic about the people in the market, who are going about their perfectly ordinary activities, buying and selling, arguing and courting, strolling and lounging. When they finish whatever they came to the market to do, they will go back to their separate worlds—to American ranch-style houses, slum shanties, old-fashioned wooden bungalows, military barracks, housing projects, farms, monastery cells, student dormitories, Chinese shop-houses, floating houses on a *klong*. For this moment in time, though, they are involved in an activity that is both strikingly contemporary and profoundly ancient—something that has been going on since the day the Emerald Buddha first crossed the river to its new home, and that is likely to go on as long as the city survives. If Bangkok has a heart, a center at once human and symbolic, a place where its myriad streams of life converge and find a unified expression, it is almost certainly here in this great marketplace.

Young men admiring a new motorbike

Movie theater on Rajadamnern Avenue decorated in honor of the king's birthday. *Right,* traffic policemen and one of Bangkok's numerous movie posters

ROSANNA
JOHN RICHARDS
"THE NUN
CROSSROA
ที่ เฉลิมเขตร์
ฉายวันนี้

The most popular movies, advertised all over the city on gigantic billboards, are the action-packed variety with plenty of bullets and blood

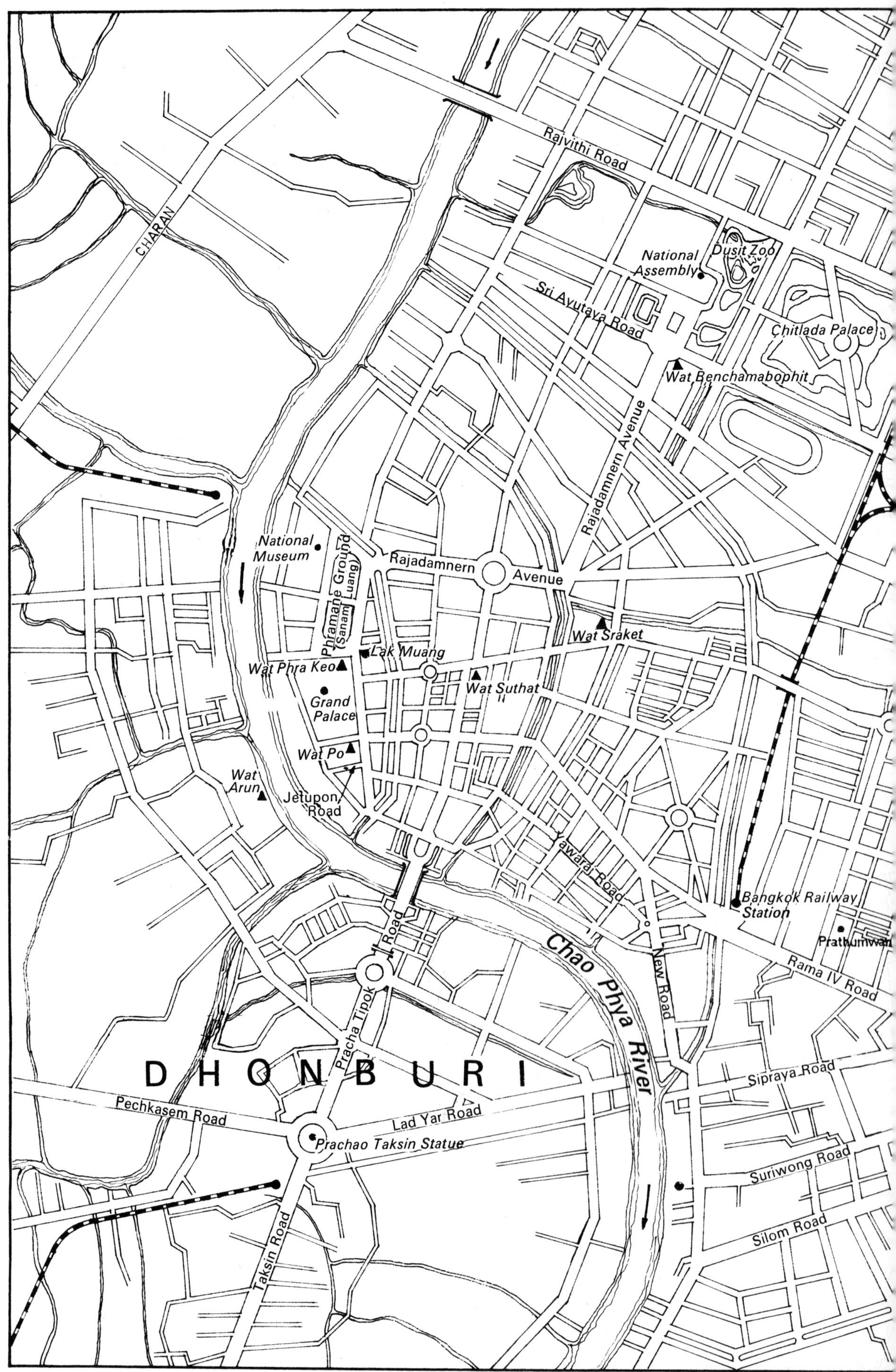

Rajvithi Road
CHARAN
National Assembly
Dusit Zoo
Sri Ayutaya Road
Chitlada Palace
Wat Benchamabophit
Rajadamnern Avenue
National Museum
Phramane Ground (Sanam Luang)
Rajadamnern
Avenue
Wat Sraket
Lak Muang
Wat Phra Keo
Wat Suthat
Grand Palace
Wat Po
Wat Arun
Jetupon Road
Yawaraj Road
Bangkok Railway Station
Prathumwan
Road
Chao Phya River
New Road
Rama IV Road
Pracha Tipok
DHONBURI
Sipraya Road
Pechkasem Road
Lad Yar Road
Prachao Taksin Statue
Suriwong Road
Silom Road
Taksin Road

BANGKOK

N
Pahol Yotin Road
Rama VI Road
Pramongkutklao Hospital
Rajvithi Road
Mittapap Road
Raj Prarop Road
Sri Ayutaya Road
PHRANAKORN
Petchburi Road
New Petchburi Road
Japanese Embassy
Road
Pavatai
Rama I Road
British Embassy
Erawan Hotel
Royal Bangkok Sports Club
Chulalongkorn University
Rjadamri Road
American Embassy
German Embassy
Sukumwit Highway
to Bangkapi
Vitayu Road
Lumpini Park
Canadian Embassy
Australian Embassy
Sathorn Road
Rama IV Road
MJH

This book is a joint production of John Weatherhill, Inc., of New York and Tokyo, and Serasia Ltd., of Hong Kong. Layout and typography by Andreas Cathomas under the direction of Régis Pagnez, and with the assistance of Jean-Luc Cheval and Robert Buroni. Type composed by Asco Trade Typesetting Ltd., Hong Kong. Plates engraved and printed in offset by Nissha, Kyoto. Bound at the Okamoto Binderies, Tokyo. The typeface used is Monophoto Univers.